€20

Sir John Keane and Cappoquin House

Maynooth Studies in Local History

SERIES EDITOR Raymond Gillespie

This volume is one of five short books published in the Maynooth Studies in Local History series in 2016. Like their predecessors they range widely, both chronologically and geographically, over the local experience in the Irish past. Chronologically they span the worlds of 16th-century Westmeath to those of Waterford in the early 20th century. Geographically, they range across the length of the country from Derry and Antrim to Waterford and Mallow in County Cork. Socially they move from the landed and elite ecclesiastical society of Sir John Keane and Thomas Ward, dean of Connor, to the social position of children who lost their mother in 19th-century Mallow and trade unionism in Derry in the 20th century. In doing so they reveal diverse and complicated societies of the local past, and the range of possibilities open to anyone interested in studying that past. Those possibilities involve the dissection of the local experience in the complex and contested social worlds of which it is part as people strove to preserve and enhance their positions within their local societies. Such studies of local worlds over such long periods are vital for the future since they not only stretch the historical imagination but provide a longer perspective on the evolution of society in Ireland and help us to understand more fully the complex evolution of the Irish experience. These works do not simply chronicle events relating to an area within administrative or geographically determined boundaries, but open the possibility of understanding how and why particular regions had their own personality in the past. Such an exercise is clearly one of the most exciting challenges for the future and demonstrates the vitality of the study of local history in Ireland.

Like their predecessors these five short books are reconstructions of the socially diverse worlds of the poor as well as the rich, women as well as men, children as well as adults and reconstruct the way in which those who inhabited those worlds lived their daily lives, often little affected by the large themes that dominate the writing of national history. In addressing these issues, studies such as those presented in these short books, together with their predecessors, are at the forefront of Irish historical research and represent some of the most innovative and exciting work being undertaken in Irish history today. Like the other volumes in this series, they provide models that others can follow, and convey the vibrancy and excitement of the world of Irish local history today.

Maynooth Studies in Local History: Number 127

Sir John Keane and Cappoquin House in time of war and revolution

Glascott J.R.M. Symes

FOUR COURTS PRESS

Set in 10pt on 12pt Bembo by
Carrigboy Typesetting Services for
FOUR COURTS PRESS LTD
7 Malpas Street, Dublin 8, Ireland
www.fourcourtspress.ie
and in North America for
FOUR COURTS PRESS
c/o ISBS, 920 N.E. 58th Avenue, Suite 300, Portland, OR 97213

ISBN 978–1–84682–613–9

Printed in Ireland
by eprint, Dublin.

Contents

Acknowledgments

This study is based on my thesis for the MA in Historic House Studies at Maynooth University. I am most grateful to my supervisor, Dr Terence Dooley, for his generous advice and encouragement.

The work would not have been possible without the whole-hearted support of Sir Charles and Lady Corinne Keane.

My thanks are due to my wife Adrienne and children Richard, Peter, Sarah and Emily who supported me throughout.

Introduction

Cappoquin House, sometimes known as Belmont after the townland in which it is located, is on an elevated site above the town of Cappoquin, Co. Waterford, and commands a view of a dramatic bend in the river Blackwater. Just visible to the west is the spectacularly sited Lismore Castle, in the ownership of the dukes of Devonshire, and to the south lies Dromana, home of the Villiers-Stuart family. The house was constructed on the site of an Elizabethan house built by the Munster planter, Sir Christopher Hatton. The building and original decoration of the late 18th-century house, commissioned by John Keane, later 1st baronet, is poorly documented. Family tradition ascribes the date of building to 1779 but no documentary evidence has come to light.

The town of Cappoquin owes its origin to early settlers who travelled up the Blackwater and it contains archaeological evidence at Lefanta, near the town, of habitation for at least 7,000 years.[1] Its steep banks were of strategic importance over the centuries and in more peaceful times its beauty led to the building of many great 18th- and 19th-century houses such as Ballynatray, Salterbridge and Tourin. Today its natural beauty is complemented by the mature designed landscapes of these estates.

To the west of Cappoquin, Saint Carthage established a monastery at Lismore in the 7th century and in the 12th century Prince John built a castle high above the river alongside the monastic site. After the defeat of the Desmond rebellion in 1583, 42,000 acres in the area between Lismore and Youghal were granted to Walter Raleigh (c.1554–1618). In 1602 he sold a large tract of land in the Lismore area to another adventurer, Richard Boyle, 1st earl of Cork, for £1,500. The reasons for this sale are unclear but at this period Raleigh was heavily engaged both at court in London and on foreign expeditions. Lismore Castle later passed from the Boyles to the Cavendish family, dukes of Devonshire, through marriage. The Anglo-Norman FitzGeralds constructed a castle at Cappoquin overlooking a bend in the river, and another at Dromana to the south to control the tidal reaches. In 1738, the former FitzGerald castle at Cappoquin was leased by John Keane from Richard Boyle, 4th earl of Cork. While it is traditionally believed that the present Cappoquin House occupies the site of this castle, building works on the former Keane bacon factory site in the 1980s uncovered what are believed to be the castle's foundations close to the banks of the river.[2]

In 1855 the Keane estate, which extended to 11,000 acres in Cos Waterford and Tipperary, was offered for sale in the Encumbered Estates Court which had been established in 1849 to deal with estates insolvent as a result of the Famine.

John Keane, who inherited the estate in 1892, recorded that he and his mother concluded from reading old letters in the family archive that this situation was the result of poor management over two generations but that the 3rd baronet had worked with Judge Keatinge, probably his father-in-law, to clear the estate from debt.[3] By 1883 Richard Keane owned 8,909 acres in Co. Waterford, valued at £3,237.[4] Successive land acts, including the Land Purchase (Ireland) Act 1903 ('Wyndham Act'), reduced the estate from this level to under 500 acres. Subsequent land purchases by the family have restored it to a more viable acreage.

John O'Hart traces the descent of John Keane down 15 generations from Daniel O'Cahan who, in turn, he traces back to Connor, prince of Limavady, Co. Londonderry, in early medieval times. At the plantation of Ulster in 1610 the O'Cahans forfeited their lands in Co. Londonderry and moved west of the Shannon. Following the victory of King William III at the battle of the Boyne in 1690, George O'Cahan (d. *c.*1742) conformed to the Established Church, anglicized his name to Keane and entered government service as a lawyer.[5] Sir Richard Keane (d. 1736), who served as governor of Minorca, mentioned in his will that he and his father used the name O'Cahan when he was a young man.[6] George's son, John Keane (*c.*1681–1756), leased 7,313 acres at Cappoquin from Richard Boyle (1694–1753), 4th earl of Cork and 3rd earl of Burlington, on 3 July 1738 for 999 years at £500 per annum.[7] His heir, his grandson John Keane (1757–1829), subsequently bought out the lease, reputedly when the Boyles needed funds for the building of Burlington House in London but this is unlikely as it had been completed some 50 years earlier. He served as member of parliament for Bangor (1791–1801) in the Irish parliament and then for Youghal (1801–6 and 1807–18) at Westminster and he was granted the United Kingdom baronetcy of Belmont, Co. Waterford, in 1801 after the Act of Union. John was the builder of the late 18th-century mansion of Belmont (now generally known as Cappoquin House).[8]

Sir John Keane (1873–1956) was very interested in his family lineage and researched it in Trinity College library and archives such as the Royal Irish Academy and the Free Library, Birmingham, noting on one occasion that he had 'read at Trinity College library and found out I think some clue of how the O'Cahans came from Ulster to Waterford'.[9]

SIR JOHN KEANE, 5TH BARONET

John Keane was born on 3 June 1873 at 18 Rutland (now Parnell) Square, Dublin; the eldest son of Sir Richard Francis Keane, 4th baronet of Cappoquin, Co. Waterford, and his wife Adelaide Sidney, née Vance. Adelaide's father, John Vance, had been successively MP for Dublin City (1852–65) and Armagh City (1867–75). John Keane succeeded his father as 5th baronet in 1892 at the age of 19.

In 1907 he married Eleanor Lucy, daughter of Michael Hicks Beach, 1st earl St Aldwyn. Hicks Beach (1837–1916) had twice served as chief secretary for Ireland (1874–8 and 1886–7) and was chancellor of the exchequer in Lord Salisbury's administration. The Keanes had four children: Adelaide Mary (b. 1907), Richard Michael, later 6th baronet (b. 1909), Sheila (b. 1911) and Madelaine Lucy (b. 1913). John died on 30 January 1956.[10]

This short book will look at Sir John Keane's military service in the British army, his public life in Ireland, both locally and nationally, and consider how it may have led to the burning of Cappoquin House during the Irish Civil War. It will examine the architecture and decoration of Cappoquin House and, following its destruction, the obtaining of compensation and its careful reconstruction. It will make use of Keane's diaries and letters to follow his military career, in particular his active service, to discover his evolving attitude to the momentous political happenings in Ireland and his role in these events, as well as the extensive correspondence relating to compensation and his management of the reconstruction of the house. These diaries, letters and papers have remained in a private archive and have not previously been available to historians.

1. John Keane and his context

This chapter will examine John Keane's education, military service and early involvement in Irish public life. It will consider how these experiences shaped his evolving political outlook. John Keane (fig. 1), like the sons of most Protestant ascendancy families, was educated in England. He attended Clifton College, a public school near Bristol, and the Royal Military Academy, Woolwich, from 1891 to 1893.[1] On graduating he was commissioned as a lieutenant in the Royal Field Artillery. His early years of military service were spent on artillery training in England and in 1896 he was appointed aide-de-camp to George Cadogan, 5th earl Cadogan, lord lieutenant of Ireland, 1895–1902, and was based at Dublin Castle. He was able to fulfil this seasonal duty while continuing service with his regiment in England. He had to relinquish his position as aide-de-camp following the outbreak of the South African (Boer) War in 1899 where he was to see active service. He found much of military life to be tedious: 'a regular mess life would kill me in a very short time'.[2] During his period of service in England he used his free time to study law and he sat the examinations of the Middle Temple, London, being called to the bar in 1904. However, he never practised as a barrister. He was self-educated in public finance and accountancy and throughout his life campaigned for the highest standards of accounting in all of the many organizations with which he was associated, not least the British army.

John Keane (1781–1844), second son of the 1st baronet and Keane's great-granduncle, had a most distinguished military career. As a lieutenant colonel he commanded a brigade in the Peninsular war and as a major-general he was severely wounded at the battle of New Orleans. After service in the West Indies and Bombay he was promoted to lieutenant-general and given command of the British Indian Army (Army of the Indus), which consisted of 21,000 men, in the first Anglo-Afghan War (1839–42). The then emir of Afghanistan, Dost Mohammad Khan (1792–1863), had alarmed the British administration in India with his overtures to the Russians. The British determined to replace him with Shah Shuja (1786–1842), a previous ruler who had been granted asylum by the British East India Company and was deemed to be more amenable to Britain's strategic interests. Keane achieved a notable victory in capturing the heavily defended fort at Ghanzi on 23 July 1839. Dost Mohammad fled and within three days Keane entered Kabul and Shuja had regained his throne. Keane was created Baron Keane of Ghuznee and of Cappoquin in recognition of his military achievements. Within three years, after Keane's command had ended, there was an insurrection during which Shuja was assassinated and Dost Mohammed

1. Sir John Keane
(1873–1956).

regained power. The British army were forced to withdraw, suffering horrendous casualties as they retreated through mountain passes in winter. The first Anglo-Afghan War has been described as Britain's greatest humiliation of the 19th century.[3]

CO-OPERATIVE MOVEMENT

Keane's first public involvement in Irish affairs was with the co-operative movement. Sir Horace Plunkett (1854–1932) advocated co-operation in 1889, drawing on an earlier experiment by Co. Clare landowner John Vandeleur, who had established Ralahine Commune in 1831 based on the principles that Robert Owen (1771–1858) had applied at the New Lanark mills in Scotland. Plunkett, who was the son of a landlord, the 16th Baron Dunsany of Co. Meath, had returned from Wyoming fired with enthusiasm for co-operation as an economic policy to counter low morale and emigration among Irish small farmers and farm labourers. He established the Irish Agricultural Organization Society and published *The Irish Homestead* to disseminate his views.

In 1899 Keane set out to establish a co-operative in Cappoquin but faced strong opposition. Father Spratt, the parish priest, supported the establishment of a creamery but opposed a co-operative store. The *Waterford Star* was opposed and criticized the *Irish Homestead*, accusing Keane of waging a sinister crusade to crush his Cappoquin town tenants.[4] However, Keane did get his way eventually. By 1914 Keane was secretary of the Blackwater Valley Co-operative Agricultural Society Limited. He also played a leading role in the establishment of the co-operative bacon factory in Waterford, supervising its construction and serving as its chairman for many years.[5] Keane wrote what were to be prophetic words about Plunkett:

Certainly he has done great work in Ireland but I do not think the present generation will appreciate in a true measure his grand achievements. I leave it to posterity to immortalise him and it will be no surprise if history were to regard him as one of the greatest and most practical benefactors of our time. Now after ranching in America he has returned to Ireland, to his native country, and there in a short period of eight years established among farmers principles of thrift and industry through the recognition of the co-operative principles of self-help.[6]

In 1897 Keane and Plunkett visited Avondale, Co. Wicklow, and Keane reflected on Charles Stewart Parnell (1846–91), 'roaming around the vales and glens forming his plans for the salvation of Ireland ... such a fine but misguided genius'.[7] Following a meeting chaired by Plunkett, he wrote:

> The movement is established, the principle is now understood and all we want is good men to organize and gather what can be gained by observing the experiences of other countries far more advanced in their modes of agriculture than ourselves ... I see a future and let us hope a great and successful future.[8]

In 1913 he accompanied the Royal English Arboricultural Society on a tour of Germany. He recorded: 'Systematic management is a very striking feature ... the country has a most prosperous appearance ... agriculture seems to flourish to judge by the signs of intensive tillage ... I longed to give my fellow county councillors a sight of such things'.[9] He also used his war service in South Africa, Belgium and France to both observe farming practices and promote the principles of co-operation.

During the War of Independence the co-operatives struggled due to a combination of post-war agricultural depression and stores having to close to prevent their stock being commandeered:

> In the meantime the economic position is very serious. The farmers can sell nothing (not even beasts changed hands at the last Dungarvan fair) and there is no prospect of any immediate change ... Several Co-operative societies, Fermoy among the number, are in difficulties and a big effort is being made to save Enniscorthy. The I[rish] A[gricultural] W[holesale] S[ociety] has agreed to head up county Co-operative societies forthwith and these ought to do some good by bringing people together.[10]

In 1924, Keane records dining with Plunkett, now resident at Weybridge following the destruction of his home, and noted: 'better, much quieter and slept a lot, not half as jumpy as he used to be ... it is very sad to see him so lost and forlorn with all his possessions in a tiny flat: after all he has done for the country. It makes me sick, sad and desperate.'[11]

SOUTH AFRICAN (BOER) WAR

On 2 November 1899 Keane 'entrained guns and horses' from the Royal Field Artillery camp in Coventry and on the next day they received 'a most hearty send off from the Coventry people' to the singing of Rule Britannia as they departed for Liverpool. They sailed the following day and before reaching Queenstown (now Cobh) they encountered bad weather and were having 'a hard time with the horses – many were ill'. In Queenstown he found enough time to travel by pony and trap to Fota to dine with the Smith-Barrys.[12] Both men and horses suffered on the journey, leading to disciplinary issues: 'Driver Young refused to obey me moreover and used most obscene language towards me … put him back for court martial. As he was being led away he turned upon me with a knife but was checked by the escort'. However, after an apology, Young was released. Eleven days after sailing nine horses were dead. After brief stops in Tenerife and Cape Town they landed in the Eastern Cape to join the battle at Molteno.[13] He witnessed men being wounded and killed in battle but almost as great a scourge was disease: 'Almost every day now we have a funeral of some sort'.[14] On 21 June 1900, he narrowly avoided injury when a bullet passed through his diary shortly after he had put it down.[15]

There were frequent lulls in the campaign and long distance to be travelled. Many areas were unaffected by fighting and officers had opportunities for social activities such as shooting game, playing polo and attending balls. Writing from Durban to his mother in August 1900, Keane said: 'I have invested in some curios as I think it a pity to return home without something typical of the country. I know you want a nice carriage ring so I bought a really fine and rather expensive one which might reach you in course of time.'[16] Keane made use of his time to learn about agricultural practices as well as promoting the principles of co-operation abroad. While camped on the veldt, he used his negotiations with Boer farmers over grazing for his horses and provisions to discuss farming. He observed:

> gave Halse the '99 [1899] report of our co-op movement … he appeared much interested especially in the technical treatment of barley growing. He very much doubted when the principle of mutual self-help could be applied to the agricultural interests out here … Dutch are anti-progress … content to exist like many Irish … in no way desirous of social or economic improvement.[17]

During the campaign Keane was promoted to captain in 1900 and in 1901 was mentioned in despatches. He received both the queen's (Victoria) and king's (Edward VII) South African campaign medals with three clasps for engagements in Wittebergen, Transvaal and Cape Colony.[18] In January 1901 he wrote in his diary 'Some basic principles of army reform'. He promoted efficiency in all organizations with which he was associated and this was to be a theme of his future military service: much later he got the opportunity to have his voice heard when he was posted to the War Office. During the 1900 general election he lamented that war service prevented him from being in Dublin to canvas for his friend and colleague in the co-operative movement, Horace Plunkett: 'It is too dreadful to be stuck in this dead and alive country [South Africa] while causes [of] such importance are occurring at home'.[19]

From 1902 to 1905 Keane served as private secretary to the Limerick-born Sir Henry Blake (1840–1918), governor of Ceylon (now Sri Lanka). Later, Blake was to be a prominent spokesman for southern unionist opinion and was a delegate of the Irish Unionist Alliance to the Irish Convention of 1917–18. However, Keane was on war service while Blake was politically active in Ireland.[20]

KEANE'S INHERITANCE

Keane resigned his army commission on 17 June 1908 to take up residence at Cappoquin following both his mother's death and his marriage in 1907. In 1909 he attended the Royal Agricultural College, Cirencester, to study estate management. Typically, he wrote a searching critique of the course on completion.[21] He had inherited the Cappoquin estate on the death of his father in 1892 and, like all such estates, it had come through turbulent times and was to face ever-greater challenges. Following poor harvests at the end of the 1870s the Land League became very active in Co. Waterford and a branch was established in Lismore in 1880.[22] Keane's father took a conciliatory approach to the Land Act of 1881, not shared by many of his fellow landlords, writing in a circular letter to his tenants: 'I am fully prepared to accept this land act in the spirit in which it is framed' and goes on to say that should landlord and tenants' views not harmonize he gave his full approval to his tenants to apply to the land courts for a resolution.[23]

At this time Cappoquin was among the 20 largest estates in the county with a valuation of £3,227. Curraghmore, valuation £27,705, Lismore, £15,000, and Dromana, £11,463 were by far the largest landholdings; the other estates were around the same valuation as Cappoquin. Evictions, backed up by police and army, particularly on the marquis of Waterford's Curraghmore estate, had raised tensions. The land acts of 1881 and 1885 had limited impact and came too late to calm the situation. The farm labourers, whose conditions were deplorable, were also in conflict with the middlemen farmers over wages and housing; this conflict was to re-emerge later during John Keane's stewardship.[24]

Cappoquin relied on the Keane family for a substantial amount of employment. Apart from the estate workers, over 100 men worked at Keane's Foundry and Henry Keane, John's younger brother, established a bacon factory in 1907 that employed over 200 people at its peak. The town was one of the parts of Waterford where the Irish language remained strong. The 1911 census shows that nearly 42 per cent of the population of Cappoquin were Irish speaking. In 1930, when Keane opposed compulsory Irish in the Senate, it was pointed out to him that several of his current estate workers were Irish speakers.[25]

While Keane was absent on military service the running of the Cappoquin estate was in the hands of Keane's mother, Adelaide, and a land agent, Thomas Henry Marmion, since his father's death.[26] Keane found the elderly Marmion to be rather too conservative for his progressive ideas on agriculture and forestry, noting that: 'He lives very much in a groove and reluctantly accepts my new proposals'.[27] He kept in regular contact with his estate by letter and visited Cappoquin whenever possible.

SOCIAL LIFE AND HOME MAKING

Throughout Keane's long life he enjoyed a hectic and energetic lifestyle filled with both work and social activities. Like most of his class he took part in field sports: riding, hunting, polo, shooting and occasional fishing. He played tennis and squash regularly; attended race meetings in Ireland and England; watched cricket at Lords and tennis at Wimbledon when in London; and attended rugby internationals both in Dublin and London. When resident in Dublin he was an all-the-year-round swimmer at the Forty-Foot bathing place near Dun Laoghaire. An energetic walker, often covering the 11 miles between Dungarvan station and Cappoquin, he also cycled and had a motorbike for a period.

As a young officer he frequently attended house parties, dinners and dances in both Great Britain and Ireland. These social occasions gave him access to many significant formers of political opinion such as Geoffrey Dawson (1874–1944), editor of the *The Times*, and John Pentland Mahaffy (1839–1919), provost of Trinity College Dublin. Music, theatre and opera were other interests and he took singing lessons for many years: he sang in church choirs and at private gatherings. He enjoyed the company of women and recorded in his diary impressions of those he met. He often commented on the intellectual quality of their conversation and he was favourable towards women having professional careers. Of one girl he observed: 'Miss Stanley is the world' and of another: 'She is a very smart looking girl and so these nonsensical views are all the more pitiable and perhaps in some cases dangerous'. He found the girls at a war-time ball in South Africa to be 'so so'. A lady, referred to as 'M', analysed his character for him and, while he admitted that a lot was true, he contended that her analysis of his attitude to marriage was entirely wrong in suggesting that to 'gratify my ambition I would secure money at the risk of my own happiness and what is most important that of another' while in fact 'My abhorrence of a worldly match is so intense that to know that a girl has money is sufficient to create quite a prejudice in my mind against her.'[28]

2. Cappoquin House, west end.

He first met Eleanor Hicks Beach while serving in England and recorded 'Miss Hicks Beach is a nice sort of girl'. He visited her home within days and noted that the family were 'very nice kind simple people. Certain society would call them dull, the reason being they are not fast. They appear to have nice taste, to be well read, interested in what goes on around them'. They might have been considered not 'fast' by not participating in the house parties of the Edwardian period that often involved drinking and gambling.[29] On 14 February 1907 the marriage of John and Eleanor took place in St Margaret's Church, Westminster, having been postponed for two days due to the sudden death of John's mother. Shortly after settling at Cappoquin they embarked on the modernization of the services in the house. An acetylene lighting plant was installed in 1910 and this necessitated the redecoration of the house the following year. Estimates were obtained for plasterwork restoration in the drawing room that was not carried out at this time; however, new architraves and shutters appear to have been supplied for the windows together with festoon blinds.[30]

In 1913 Keane commissioned Page Dickinson (1881–1958) of Orpen and Dickinson, architects, Dublin, to replace a Regency veranda with a more substantial portico (fig. 2). Both Keanes were actively involved in the detailed design work for the project. Keane was concerned by Dickinson's use of iron girders covered by only six inches of concrete but was reassured that this was now common practice and that there would be no problems with water ingress. The simple, classical-style portico with pediment blended well with the house and the use of old millstones in the paving, presumably from the estate, was a surprising arts-and-crafts touch. Dickinson opted for piers rather than pillars in order not to 'show up the plainness of the old work'.[31] At the same time a scheme of decorative plaster was designed and executed in the drawing room, with two Dublin firms and Jackson of London being asked to quote. The contract was won by M. Creedon of Dublin. Keane was always very conscious of costs and queried Creedon's estimate and even suggested to Dickinson that hollow concrete piers in the portico might reduce costs.

A slight mystery surrounds the impetus for this new decorative scheme as the detailed correspondence between architect and client makes it clear that the intention was to replicate lost stucco work, some evidence of which apparently still existed on the walls and of which Keane had an old photograph. Dickinson was a connoisseur of 18th-century plaster decoration: later he was co-author of *Georgian mansions of Ireland*.[32] A carpenter, J.W. Daly, provided an estimate for repairs to doors and for new window sashes.[33] (New window architraves and shutters had been fitted a few years before.) One can only speculate as to whether there had been a fire in the room or if the decoration had been altered previously. Renovation would have been natural with the change of generations and installation of new services but it is possible that land sales under the Wyndham Act may have supplied the necessary funds.

The Keane's four children were born between 1909 and 1914 and the family enjoyed a lively social life in Waterford, Dublin and London. Among their friends were the London society portrait-painter Maurice W. Greiffenhagen RA (1862–1931) and his wife. The Griffenhagens were guests in Waterford in 1913 and Maurice painted a pair of portraits of John and Eleanor (figs 3&4), dressed in informal country wear, at a cost of £150 each. The portraits were exhibited in the Royal Hibernian Academy in 1923, as Keane records the family went 'to RHA and saw our portraits'.[34] Greiffenhagen most likely carried out other commissions as he stayed for at least a month; he visited Tourin where it is possible Sir R. Musgrave sat for him. However, the family's tranquillity was to be short lived due to events both in Ireland and in Europe.

Keane demonstrated a strong Christian faith throughout his life and was a regular Sunday worshipper, sometimes morning and evening, in the Church of Ireland. He frequently noted the theme of the sermon in his diary and whether he agreed with the theology or otherwise. He served on both the general synod and representative body of the Church of Ireland and was a governor of several church-related institutions.

He appears to have enjoyed good relations with his Roman Catholic neighbours and employees. In 1897, he provided a site for a convent and school on demesne lands on favourable terms. He agreed to let the land with: 'Half an acre free, remaining land at £3 per acre'.[35] This was in the family tradition

3. Maurice Greiffenhagen, RA, John Keane.

4. Maurice Greiffenhagen, RA, Eleanor Keane.

as Richard Keane had assisted the Cistercian order establish their monastery at Mount Melleray by offering 500 acres of reclaimable mountain land at reduced terms in 1832. In 1820, a previous John Keane had provided the site for the first Roman Catholic church in Cappoquin.[36] Census figures show that when John Keane inherited Cappoquin the resident household staff of eight were all Roman Catholics, except for the governess and one maid, as would have been almost all of the estate workers.[37]

DEVELOPING A POLITICAL PHILOSOPHY

On 16 May 1897 Keane wrote in his diary: 'I hope to try and establish as my guiding factor through my public life; my country and the welfare of my people first and principles and standards of public honesty first ... Thus and thus alone can any man do justice to both his public and his private morals.'[38] Keane harboured political ambitions and frequently attended debates in the House of Commons when he was in London, observing in 1899 that he was 'more confident than ever that I should be satisfied with my career if I was in the House of Commons, but how to get there is the difficulty. Yet one can generally achieve anything on which one sets one's heart'.[39] He attended many political meetings as he began to form his own political philosophy.

The *Waterford Star* reported his coming-of-age in 1894 when he was welcomed to Cappoquin with floral arches and an address:

> Of course he is a gentleman young in years and of necessity limited experience but, nevertheless he is sufficiently old and discriminating to realize the meaning and import of such a greeting where priest and parson and all classes in the district in a glorious Home Rule spirit so heartily doing honour on so felicitous an occasion. He has great opportunities for acquiring the affection and gratitude of the people, and let us hope for his own and his family's sake he will utilize them worthily and well.[40]

The hosting of a Conservative Party Primrose League ball at this period brought a response from the same paper that gave him an early warning of the political atmosphere he would encounter at home: they said they would have advocated a boycott of the ball if they had known its Conservative nature in advance as they:

> have a duty to perform in protesting against Nationalists allowing themselves to be made effusive toadies or undiscerning flatterers of any family, be their position what it may, that panders to the perpetuation of the evictor's tyranny or the domination of a class that has been Ireland's greatest curse and scourge.[41]

He appears to have gradually moved away from a Conservative, unionist position as he realized that a more radical Irish policy was necessary. In 1895 he had written in connection with a speech made by Arthur Balfour (1848–1930), future Conservative prime minister, 'I thought very fine and certainly to anybody gifted with ordinary common sense the unionist policy must appear the only sound one'. He attended a meeting addressed by Joseph Chamberlain (1836–1914), who became a Liberal Unionist following disagreement with Gladstone over home rule.[42] In 1898 he attended a rally in Birmingham addressed by Herbert H. Asquith (1852–1928), future Liberal prime minister, 'I was pleased with his speech as a radical performance … The glorious traditions of the liberal party.'[43]

In 1897, he looked back on what he felt had been lost opportunities with respect to Irish policy:

> One is almost reduced to tears to think of the opportunities that we better class has allowed to slip away. We have through our want of foresight and more appreciation of the near future sanctioned a national party to spring up and champion the cause of Ireland which when resolved into its component parts repels the true instinct of right-minded men. The National party might have been a noble party comprising intellect, brains, and wealth … Even Parnell in late years gave the lead, a master mind whom the proprietary class might have well and honestly trusted … Ireland by a large national majority demands self-government. The right is denied on account of the insecure guarantee as to the safeguards for the intellectual and proprietary minority. This minority is rapidly approaching extinction. *Ergo* the present majority must finally prevail since the demands will be unanimous.[44]

While staying at a house party at Haddo, Scotland, the home of the Hamilton-Gordons in the following year, Ishbel, Lady Aberdeen, whose husband had served as a Liberal lord lieutenant of Ireland in 1886 and was to so serve again from 1905 to 1915, urged him to stand as a radical and he observed that she:

> admitted in favour of Home Rule in theory and said that the present conditions in Ireland made it a dangerous experiment to grant them powers of self-government … I do not for a moment think she is the dangerous person people say she is and probably all said and done her reforms would, if carried out, do little harm to the State and Empire. She certainly is the ruling power in the household and guides Lord Aberdeen in political matters. Of one thing I am certain she is thoroughly sincere and is activated by the highest motives.[45]

When serving as ADC to Cadogan he observed of the lord lieutenant and Gerald Balfour (1853–1945), the chief secretary, that 'neither of them … know

much about the country and yet they are both clever men'. He goes on to refer
to the introduction of laws:

> instituted by a class differing in religion, nationality, and sympathy and
> working in complete disregard of the people ... the harmony between
> Protestant and Catholic, between master and man <u>can</u> be brought about
> but only by time and prudence, by considerate legislation and by due
> regard to the national character on the part of Englishmen who may be
> sent to this country to represent imperial government.[46]

Keane recorded a conversation during which Cadogan put forward the
suggestion that the:

> most wholesome lesson for the country would be complete alienation
> from England for a few years. No alliance with any foreign power would
> be allowed and no financial support would be given by the richer country.
> Then this country would come to appreciate its poverty and absolute
> inability to govern, and an alliance with England would be only too
> readily welcomed.[47]

This perhaps illustrates something of the British administration's lack of understanding of the realities of the situation. Keane's opinions on home rule seem
to waver from expressing support to Lady Aberdeen in 1899 to his 1912 diary
entry: 'I do not like Home Rule but see the complete failure of the union and
as we are at present our people can never be self-respecting and our politicians
anything but obstructionists'. Yet, in 1913, he wrote a letter to the editor of the
Irish Times in which he stated: 'I am a strong believer in Home Rule'.[48]

Keane regretted not having had a university education and devoted much
of his spare time to self-education in the classics and political philosophy. His
reading of law was part of his preparation for a political career in England and
a possible fall-back 'should army still disgust'.[49] Ultimately, he could not decide
whether he wanted to stand as a Conservative or a Liberal Unionist and thought
that he would not be able to obtain a nomination for an English seat in any
event. He does not appear to have considered standing in an Irish constituency
at any time.[50]

Early in 1914, probably in the context of the developing split between
southern and northern unionists, he was pessimistic regarding the future for
Ireland, writing:

> The general political unrest is most disquieting and the outlook gloomy,
> not so much on account of civil war but the prospect of settling the
> question of the exclusion of Ulster. This unhappy country promises to
> be eternally in the hands of agitators when proper responsibility might
> easily cure.[51]

In an undated article preserved in his scrapbook, which he wrote prior to 1922 for some publication under the title 'Ireland as an Irishman sees her' he said: 'Looking to the future, there is one feature which seems to stand clear and striking out of the whole confusion and conflicting uncertainties. That is the absolute necessity for a united Ireland for future success.' Later in 1914 he broke his diary and wrote his 'reflections':

> The party machine is working its worst … a game between haves and have nots, Orange man and Hibernian, professional and professing politician, and all fought over the body of poor Ireland …What is right each person must decide for himself according to his inner convictions and there is no better guide than that of Christian principle … Honesty is not the best, it is the only policy.[52]

Soon he was also pessimistic for the future of Europe: 'War between Austria and Serbia and very serious news and most likely serious European complications'.[53] These events were to divert him from Irish affairs for the next four years.

WATERFORD COUNTY COUNCIL

In 1911, Keane was elected to Waterford County Council and during this period he became allied to William O'Brien's All-for-Ireland League.[54] O'Brien (1852–1928) served as a Nationalist MP for various Munster constituencies between 1883 and 1918. Following the split in the Nationalist party after the fall of Parnell, he established the league in 1909 to campaign for dominion-status home rule by agreement between nationalists and unionists, through his '3 Cs' – conference, conciliation, consent. O'Brien set out the aims of the League as:

> the union and active co-operation in every department of our national life of all Irish men and women who believe in the principles of domestic self-government for Ireland … the surest means to be a combination of all elements of the Irish population in a spirit of mutual tolerance and patriotic goodwill, such as shall guarantee to the Protestant minority of our fellow-countrymen inviolable security for all their rights and liberties, and win the friendship of the people of Great Britain without distinction of party.[55]

In 1910, O'Brien's *Cork Free Press* had asked of the landlords: 'as a class is it not unfortunate that you for the most part are outside the political life of your country.'[56] In 1914, Keane spoke at a League conference in Cork and recalled the spirit of 1798, going on to say, that this spirit had 'made Ulster the masters of the present situation, and if we had that spirit we would be in the same position ourselves.'[57] For a short period the League enjoyed the support of a number of Munster MPs, landowners and businessmen. O'Brien considered partition to be too high a price to pay for home rule and Keane would have been in total sympathy with his rejection of violence, landlord-tenant conciliation and, probably by this time, home rule by consent. In 1918, on learning that George Russell (AE, 1853–1919), an associate of Plunkett in the co-operative movement, had resigned from the Landlords' Convention, he wrote: 'I suppose the possible settlement is not sufficiently extreme for him. I should be satisfied with settlement on a federal basis though I think a dominion status will be more satisfactory'.[58]

Keane was a diligent member of the county council and served as a guardian of the Lismore Poor Law Union responsible for running the workhouse. He gave his attention to a wide range of matters and always insisted on strict adherence to procedural rules, to best accountancy practices and, especially, to the proper running of the workhouse. A diary entry in 1912 following a county council meeting expresses his frustration with the petty rivalries of local politics: 'one is up against a whole national system caring little for public and much for private interests'.[59] In the year that he was first elected to the county council he was also appointed high sheriff of Co. Waterford – a position that had been held by both his father and grandfather.

WORLD WAR

Early in August 1914 the mobilization of the British army was ordered and Keane, now 41 years old, travelled to England as a member of the Officers' Reserve to set about the task of shipping men and horses to France. During a brief visit home he found time to give a lecture on the war in Cappoquin and on 12 August he wrote: 'orders to embark tomorrow. Such a rush, and very hard work to bear up saying goodbye to children.'[60] Prior to leaving for the front Keane had housed 40 to 50 Belgian refugees in Cappoquin.[61] It appears that they quickly moved on to employment in English munitions' factories. A much smaller group arrived early in 1915 and Keane wrote to his wife: 'I am glad the Belgians have arrived safely. You might find them some work at Cappoquin if they are skilled cabinet makers'.[62] This was to be repeated in 1939 when the Keanes accommodated Austrians in Ardmore who were from among the Jewish refugees brought to Ireland by Hubert Butler (1900–91).

Keane embarked for France on 13 August and saw active service in the fighting around Ypres. Here he experienced the horrors of trench warfare when he had to visit observation posts at the front that were targeting heavy guns that were in the second line. He recorded: 'I saw one German quite plainly over the trench and gave him a round'; 'They just brought in … one of the 28th Brigade batteries with both legs blown off. Poor chap he will die very soon and

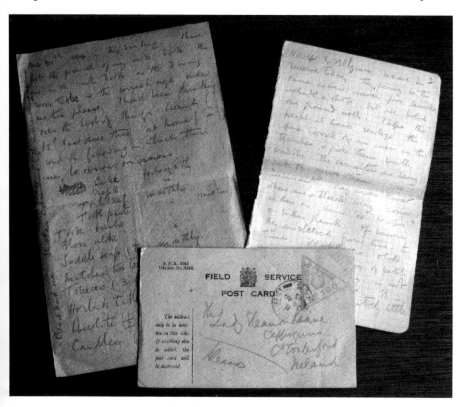

5. First World War letters from John to Eleanor Keane.

the sooner the better'; 'In front of our trenches the bodies of 14 Frenchmen killed in an attack some weeks ago can be seen with the naked eye' and 'I hear the town of Ypres, one of the finest in Flanders and full of gems of architecture, is flat. The destruction of war is appalling'.[63] One of his major concerns was his horses: 'The horses in our battery are looking very well – surprisingly so. They never see a stable of course and are often standing in mud' and 'The French told me they literally had a horse drowned in mud'. He frequently lamented the long-term damage done to the landscape by the horses through the 'barking' of trees.[64]

The same conditions also affected the men: 'They have had 300 to 400 men invalided from some of his regiments owing to what they call neuritis of the feet. Inflammation of the nerves due to cold bed and being unable to move them in the sodden ground, all this as the result of one night's work!' Keane witnessed the early use of gas in the prolonged and fierce fight to hold the Ypres salient, the area around the town that was surrounded by German-held territory: 'One shell last night was a stinker, most unpleasant, and my eyes did smart and water'.

He was often exposed to shell fire and recorded a 'near miss' and posted the splinter home as it might 'amuse the children'. He wrote, 'Napoleon's old saying that the day of battle is the soldiers' holiday is not true of modern war. It is all battle and comparatively little marching.'[65]

Keane lost his diary in February 1915 in Belgium and from then on recorded his experiences in almost daily letters to his wife, Lady Eleanor (fig. 5). (Most of them were typed up later.) He devised a cypher to inform her of place names as field post was subject to censorship. When he found himself as prosecutor at the court martial of a man who persisted in writing home the 'most insubordinate letters', Keane observed to his wife 'Do you think that charges might be made against me?'[66] Through his friendship with Geoffrey Dawson, editor of the *The Times*, some of his reports were published under the title 'From the front: an artillery captain's journal of the war'.

Writing to his wife in December he said:

> The firing is the same as ever, never five seconds without a shot, but we hold our ground well. I hope the people at home realize the fine work of our men in the trenches and give them full credit. The casualties are heavy but the nerve strain is incessant … I do wish a party of representative men, Irish as well as English, could be sent here to see the devastation of war … If the Germans ever do raid England or Ireland, I shall have no pity for those who have sat at home and done nothing but grumble … I want you to get extracts from my letters published.[67]

Despite the horrors of war there were glimpses of normality – although far fewer than in his accounts of South Africa – such as aristocratic French officers producing bottles of champagne with their own chateaux on the label, the daily lives of civilians trying to survive just behind the lines and opportunities for shopping: 'They make very good lace in Ypres and I must try and get you some, but there is a great run on it, and prices have doubled.' The next day: 'I am sending you some lace which I bought this morning.'[68]

In late 1915 and in 1916 he was instructing young officers in the use of newly introduced trench mortars at the Second Army Trench Mortar School at Turdegham, Hazebrouck, French Flanders. He was mentioned in despatches in 1915, and promoted to major in 1916, being awarded the Distinguished Service Order in the same year. From 1917 to the end of the war he was in the War Office in London working on weapons development.[69] In 1917 he was awarded the *Legion d'honneur* by the French government and he ended the war with the rank of lieutenant-colonel.[70]

On 6 August 1914 Keane had written to the *Irish Times* urging his fellow-countrymen 'to pull together without prejudice to their political opinions' so that after the war 'political differences are not so acute as they appeared in the past'.[71] Like John Redmond (1856–1918), and many of his compatriots, he hoped that the war would unite Irishmen and lead to home rule by consent. On learning of the 1916 Rising he wrote to his wife: 'They seem to have had a lot of fighting in Dublin. I imagine the rebels were full of drink. I see they looted the shops in the most wholescale manner. The authorities seem to have been entirely unprepared at which I am not surprised.'[72] He agreed with a letter to the *The Times* from Lord Hugh Cecil, a conservative opponent of home rule: 'the most sensible statement we have had on the Irish question. His method is the stick all round (he does not say [Edward] Carson included) and he is right'.[73] In 1917 he wrote of rumours of a forecast of: 'a Seinn [*sic*] Fein rising and massacre of the Protestants or unionists is very disturbing and I should think very unlikely unless the government gives up all idea of governing.'[74]

During the war years his wife had to assume a major role in the management of the Cappoquin estate, which besides the house included garden, home farm, forestry, tree nursery, saw mill and tenants leases. Keane insisted on regular detailed reports and sent very specific instructions regarding the farm. In February 1915 he wrote: 'I hope careful consideration will be given to the question of next year's crops. It might be advisable to grow rather more grain – possibly some wheat – than our working plan normally contemplates' and in March: 'I am very distressed to hear another heifer has aborted ... I feel dirt is the chief cause and we must tackle the matter resolutely ... get the Dep[artmen]t leaflet on the subject. It is a matter of disinfecting the premises'. In April he wrote: 'I imagine the labour question must be getting serious with so many gone to the war. You may find women quite satisfactory in the garden' and in June 1916: 'I am looking forward anxiously to your farm balance sheet'.[75]

As in South Africa, he used his service in the First World War to observe agricultural methods. In February 1915 he wrote:

> I am very busy now preparing an account for the *Homestead* [magazine of the Co-operative Society] of a typical Belgian Farm. I have pumped the owner of this farm dry and am giving details of his crops, his labour, his stock, how he lives, a kind of Arthur Young inquiry which may be of some interest at home.[76]

He found the farms to be highly productive with the farmers working long hours, observing to his wife: 'They work from 4.30 to 8, breakfast of meat, coffee, etc., 8.30–12, another meat meal; 1.30–6, coffee, bread and butter, 6.30–8, 12 hours actual work.'[77] On 2 November 1914 he recorded:

> We are again in much cultivated and thickly populated country. The farm buildings are substantial and they live much better than our farmers do ... Had we not been hurried away, I meant to have spent a day at our last place, collecting exact particulars of area, yield, implements etc., on a typical farm which we occupied and of which 90% appeared to be

tillage. I am much struck by the number of implements used. This farm is about 80 acres, has a binder and mower, a thrashing machine, and a large assortment of cultivating implements. Their ploughs seems older fashioned than ours, and I have not seen a disc harrow. Their carts are peculiar. Three wheels one in the centre like a tricycle.[78]

Later that month he wrote home:

> I have great farming talks with the people here. They are very interested in all I tell them. They always feed their pigs on cooked food and now fuel is so scarce I am advising them to try the same uncooked which we find at home just as good. They are going to do so. They threshed wheat yesterday, a portable engine, an English thresher, a trusser (like we have and never use) and a large number of men mostly refugees.[79]

Keane's final reflection as he prepared to return to civilian life in March 1919 was: 'I am looking forward with great joy to joining my family on Tuesday. I feel I do not really know any of them now. Whatever the future may produce let us turn the present to best account.'[80]

Two of Keane's brothers, Lieutenant-Colonel Richard Henry (Harry) Keane (1881–1925) and Captain George Michael Keane (1875–1957), Royal Navy, also served in the war. Lady Eleanor Keane's brother, Michael Hicks Beach, was killed in action in Egypt in 1916. Towards the close of the war a Cappoquin estate worker, Fred, joined John in France working in army workshops casting hand grenades. It seems likely that he had acquired these skills in the Keane foundry although there are references to him having been a fisherman.

Upon returning home after the war, Keane was determined to adopt the latest agricultural innovations. This was reflected in his involvement with the co-operative movement. He was undoubtedly influenced by his experiences on active military service and his involvement in local government had given him an insight into the growing confrontation between unionist and nationalist and a realization that the political *status quo* was becoming untenable.

2. Wars and revolution at home

In this chapter Keane's role in the Irish Farmers' Union during the farm workers' strike is examined as are the effects of the War of Independence and the Civil War on the Cappoquin estate and the Keane family. The consequences of his involvement in the Free State and its first Senate are also considered.

In 1919 the War of Independence broke out and the RIC was reinforced by temporary constables recruited in Britain, known as the 'Black and Tans' and also by 'Auxiliaries', paramilitary police drawn from the British army. Hostilities continued until the signing of a truce in July 1921. Munster was the scene of some of the worst violence.[1] Thomas Kelleher of Cappoquin recalled that by 1917 the IRA was holding weekly parades in a field rented from Keane as a hurling pitch and Michael O'Donoghue of Lismore refers to an arms dump on the Cappoquin demesne as well as gelignite being stored in the Keane-owned foundry in the town.[2] Keane records the destruction of the Dublin Custom House: 'Yes, the poor Custom House: our greatest architectural joy; madness I call it: you do not paralyse government by such tactics: in fact the burning of papers probably does good. I know a fire at the War Office would do the army infinite good'.[3]

In 1921, writing while in London, he stated:

> It is not till the IRA levy is made upon me that there is any real risk of violence – this levy has not been made yet and it is unlikely to be made except on me in person. The longer it can be put off the better and now the Ulster Parliament is in operation and the military measures are to be stronger, bottom may be touched any day. Wood [agent at Lismore Castle] says the risk of burning is just as great, if not greater, when I am at home than away.[4]

Returning to Dublin after the truce he wrote: 'I do not find any exultation here over the Truce and the chief enthusiasm among the street Arabs which were collecting pennies to "burn a black and tan", in effigy I presume. It is sad to see how guily [sic – guilefully?] some regard the future'. Keane's own observation on the truce was: 'this morning the announcement of peace whatever that means and now the press, especially Irish, will be busy making the proper atmosphere. I am relieved but do not rejoice. They will find that peace is harder than war, as Lloyd George has already found.'[5]

CIVIL WAR

Neither the truce of 11 July 1921 nor the Anglo-Irish Treaty of 6 December 1921 were to bring tranquillity to either the Keane family or the country. The Irish Free State came into being on 6 December 1922 and its birth was marked by the outbreak of civil war waged by Republicans, who had rejected the treaty, against the National Army of the new state. The Republicans were opposed to the partition of the country and the retention of the British sovereign as head of state rather than an all-Ireland, independent republic. Keane was frequently in Dublin on business during the Civil War and was a witness to many of the events of the time. In January 1922 he witnessed the military evacuation of Dublin Castle:

> I found a crowd yesterday outside the Castle watching the evacuation, mostly youths and unemployed. I was mistaken for a Britisher and booed! ... the general feeling up here is that Labour is arranging opposition with de Valera and the other extremists with the object of obtaining a soviet government. The *Voice of Labour* is talking after the way of Moscow.[6]

This growing fear of communism was a result of increased trade union militancy from 1913 onwards, now viewed in the light of the Russian Revolution of 1917.

The tensions of the period, particularly for those of the loyalist tradition, are clear when he wrote: 'Nellie [Eleanor] and I alone at Cappoquin with only two servants ... the country is in a state of anarchy and we are preparing for a siege' and: 'Times are nerve racking. Every day one or more problems arising out of lawlessness. It may be good for the wits but it is trying to the nerves'.[7] In January 1923, the *Irish Times* reported that a ship with munitions bound for Cappoquin had been apprehended and that all the bridges below had recently been destroyed.[8] In June a Mr Bishop approached Keane asking him: 'to go with him and ask [Winston] Churchill what England is going to do if the Treaty breaks down.'[9] When in Dublin on 28 June 1922 he almost casually records being woken at 4.15 a.m. by rifle and gun fire as the National Army attacked the Four Courts, which had been occupied by Republicans. He notes:

> considerable activity on streets, tenders and armoured cars, same as before Truce only Free State troops rather than British ... On my way back went down a side street, found myself in the company of some twenty others right opposite the Four Courts. A certain amount of resulting sniping and occasional rounds from 18 pounders. A few holes [in Four Courts] ... On the whole an exciting day but the intensity of the fighting much exaggerated and mostly casualties among civilians.

Two days later he observed 'ominous looking smoke' over the Four Courts and heard that it was on fire.[10]

In August, back in Cappoquin, he noted some of the effects of the Civil War. Republicans had damaged the railway bridge and attempted to destroy the Victoria (now Avonmore) road bridge, which had been built by a Keane ancestor as a famine relief measure. The next day he notes a big explosion on the bridge.[11] In July, when travelling in Co. Wexford, he reported:

> stopped by irregulars between Arklow and Gorey. A wild parcel of young enthusiast little regarding the consequences of their escapade, pleased with the spirit of adventure. The captain, a pockmarked youth of under twenty came along and talked to driver. We were asked to tell the boys in Gorey that the Arklow barracks had gone up and then we [were] allowed to pass ... An eventful week; for which all who have anything will have to pay dearly.[12]

On 23 August, his family returned home via Cork shortly after the death of Michael Collins (1890–1922) and he wrote: 'found Cork much moved over Collins death. He was killed in ambush near Macroom. He was our one hope of strong government and now the outlook is disquieting as there is no outstanding person to replace him.'[13] It might seem unusual for someone of Keane's background to speak thus of Collins given his violent role in the War of Independence but it probably reflects a genuine respect for, and faith in, his qualities of leadership. The appearance of the National Army in November did little to reassure this former army officer:

> There are a number of Free State troops in Cappoquin ... They have no semblance of soldiers except their rifles and uniform. Even the latter is mixed with civilian costume. They look about and point their rifles anywhere. It is impossible to distinguish the sentry from his comrades not on duty ... there appears to be no senior officer to visit and correct. This does not promise well.[14]

He found time to write a series of articles describing the Civil War under the title 'Ireland' for the *Edinburgh Review*.

FARM WORKERS' STRIKE

By the end of First World War the Irish Farmers' Union had established a network of provincial and local branches. While it recruited farmers of all income levels, its spokesmen were mainly large landowners formerly associated with the Irish Unionist Alliance and the Irish Landowners' Convention.[15] Keane was the chairman of the Waterford branch. Attempts to organize farm labourers had led to a series of farm workers' strikes over a number of years and by 1919 the Irish Transport and General Workers Union had established a branch in Cappoquin.[16] In the 1920s the landowners of the Blackwater valley were the focus of a protracted struggle, as by 1921 a post-war fall in the price of agricultural produce caused the employers to seek a reduction in wages. Keane was not prepared to negotiate with the ITGWU. The employers feared Bolshevism, echoing fears expressed in Dublin during the 1913 lockout, and when the provisional government was established it too was concerned about Republican support for the workers.

On 12 May 1921 Michael Banks, an ITGWU official, took over Cleeves Butter factory in Carrick-on-Suir and the communist red flag was flown. The farmers withdrew their milk supplies and eventually purchased separators to make their own butter. This led to workers raiding farms to stop butter production.[17] In 1922 the farmers attempted to cut wages by over 30 per cent and remove certain seasonal bonuses and this led to a bitter strike with Keane again speaking for the Co. Waterford employers together with Richard Musgrave of Tourin and B.J. Ussher of Cappagh. This was portrayed as a struggle between Bolshevism and Christianity.

Cappoquin demesne was to feel the full consequences of the strike:

> I heard that pickets had arrived at farm. I went up and found a dozen pickets men there including Stapleton [local strike leader] and Purcell. Told them that they had no authority to enter my place … they already had the farm men on the road. They then went and by threats but no actual violence got out the garden men. T. Quinlan and J. Boland strongly protested.[18]

Keane went to Dungarvan to speak to the IRA commandant who promised protection as and when necessary. The next day he went to milk the cows and found about 50 men around the farm: 'mainly unwilling conscripts from Dromana'.[19] The following day his tradesmen and saw-mill workers were called out. There was widespread intimidation of non-union men, which was reported in the press.[20] He then travelled to Dublin to see Patrick Hogan (1891–1936), minister for lands and agriculture, seeking protection for farmers. Hogan was 'sympathetic and angry, took notes and said he would see minister for defence [Richard Mulcahy]. He took a gloomy view of things.' He had previously discussed the situation with Arthur Griffith (1872–1922), president of the Dáil, shortly before the latter's death.[21] While in Dublin, Keane was to learn from Eleanor that 15 cattle had been driven from the farm. Three days later the cows were retrieved from Clonmel.[22]

An offer by the Devonshire estate to restore the original wage, but with reduced numbers employed, was rejected by Keane and the strike organizer. By mid-June Keane felt that he might have to sell his cattle and that the village would be without milk for the winter. A few days later he received a threatening letter and his telephone cable was cut. By August 1922 the Sinn Fein flag was flying over Lismore Castle.[23] As the strike continued farmers and traders went to Dungarvan harbour in June to unload the *Lady Belle*.[24] On 20 June he was approached with a further proposal:

> Beecher [Lismore Castle manager] turned up with some of the police from Fermoy. The chief policeman looked more like a scrap iron merchant ... suggested I should let the men go back at former wages for three months without prejudice to my rights ... require in writing from labour leaders ... he said he would procure. Beecher has become abject again and says he must surrender as he has no water.[25]

In 1923 over 500 men of the Special Infantry Corps of the National Army had to be sent to Waterford to protect farmers collecting supplies.[26] In August, Keane remained belligerent, noting that the secretary of his branch of the IFU had been wounded and stating: 'farmers as a whole inert and avaricious and they will get it in the neck before things are right'.[27] The Waterford branch of the IFU published a poster alleging that 35 cows, seized in Cappoquin from Keane, had been kept and milked for 12 weeks.[28] Keane noted that the IFU was gaining members:

> we [probably meaning the landlord leaders of the IFU] can identify with the settlement now ... I suppose de Valera and the extremists will now join the transport workers – in Wexford as one man said 75% of farmers are for a settlement and yet the four Dáil members will probably support de Valera: a sad commentary on democracy.[29]

The dispute continued into 1923 with reports of 'relations between the employers and the men appear to be becoming more strained' and: 'workers and employers who made agreements with the Irish Transport Union have had their crops pulled up'.[30] In September 1923 Keane chaired a meeting of the East and West Waterford Farmers' Protection Association at which a motion was passed stating that, due to outrages against property and claims by union officials to farmers' land, they would not deal with the ITGWU but would only deal directly with the men.[31] By December the strike had petered out: however, Keane's men had returned to work as early as July 1922, probably as a result of a local settlement at Cappoquin, Dromana and Tourin: 'The men came down to yard at 8.00 [a.m.]. They all went back to work. So the strike is over and I do not think I have lost very much.'[32]

However Keane was impressed by the young state's actions in defending the rule of law, writing:

> were it not for the protection afforded by the armed forces of the State, a bitter class war might have been precipitated. The action of the

Voice of Labour   *12 Aug 1922*

Keane's Battered Halo.

In the three other Cappoquin jobs referred to—one of them is the Dromana Estate and the other two are run by Baronets Keane and Musgrave—the employees some time ago returned to work, against the instructions of the Union, at the 30/- rate which that devoted friend and sage counsellor of the workers, Sir John Keane, had in his mind for all the Waterford labourers. It is decidedly not his fault that 90 per cent. of the men in the county have gained the full wage which they sought. The "ratting" of the employees in these three jobs is deplorable, but we have less contempt for them than we have for Keane. For his feat in humiliating his men to this degradation, he is now welcome to all the glory that is his due in this world and the next. The end is not yet, Sir John.

6. Cutting from *Voice of Labour*, 12 August 1922.

government in affording protection in a firm and impartial manner, and thus establishing the principle that any who wish to work unmolested [*sic*], is a good omen for the future of the State.[33]

These events resulted in the majority of larger farmers becoming loyal supporters of the Cumann na nGaedheal party.

The apparent victory of the IFU over the ITGWU left a legacy that may have proved costly for some, Keane in particular, in the years to come. Keane kept a cutting from the Labour Party's *Voice of Labour* in his scrapbook; it referred to Dromana, Tourin and Cappoquin with an implied threat (fig. 6):

employees some time ago returned to work, against the instructions of the union, at the 30s. rate which that devoted friend and sage counsellor of the workers, Sir John Keane, had in his mind for all the Waterford labourers. It is decidedly not his fault that 90% of the men in the county have gained the full wage they sought. The 'ratting' of the employees in these three jobs is deplorable but we have less contempt for them than we have for Keane. For his feat in humiliating his men to this degradation, he is now welcome to all the glory that is his due in this world and the next. The end is not yet, Sir John.[34]

SENATE

Keane was nominated, as an independent, to the first Senate by William T. Cosgrave (1880–1965), president of the Executive Council of the Free State, for a 12-year term in 1922. Despite his record of conscientious attendance and constructive contribution, he was not elected in 1934. From 1936 to 1938 the senate was abolished; in 1938 the taoiseach, Eamon de Valera (1882–1975), nominated him to the re-constituted Senate in which the number of nominated members was reduced to 11. He was nominated again in 1943 and 1944, serving in all for 22 years.

Keane had always seen public service as a duty so he accepted Cosgrave's offer in 1922. The block of 30 nominated senators, in a house of 60, was for the most part made up of landowners and former southern unionists: 20 were members of the Church of Ireland, three were Quakers and one was a Jew; seven were peers and five were baronets. It also included businessmen such as Henry Guinness and Andrew Jameson as well as the owner of the *Freeman's Journal*, Martin Fitzgerald, and the poet William Butler Yeats. The intention was to give a voice in the new state to a segment of society that was unlikely to gain representation by election and to provide expertise in scrutinizing legislation which might be lacking in the Dáil. Keane was probably chosen for his knowledge of agriculture, economics and business. He was often dismayed by the lack of commitment shown by many of his fellow independents: 'Much apathy among our own people many of whom do not attend.' He was also critical of the views expressed by some and stated that Maurice Moore had 'made an ass of himself' by holding up a bill granting amnesty to all persons conspiring against the State.[35]

The first Senate was very active, considering over 100 bills, a third of which were amended. The vast majority of over 500 amendments were accepted by the Dáil.[36] In July 1923 John Bagwell (1874–1946), for whom Keane had the utmost regard, said:

the southern landlords have ceased to be the backbone of the British garrison in Ireland … they have ceased even to be 'unionists', they have not ceased, however, and do not want to cease, to enrich their country with inherited gifts of loyalty and leadership and their capacity for public service.[37]

Donal O'Sullivan (1893–1973), first clerk of the Senate, later commented:

It proved that Nationalist and Unionist could work harmoniously together for the good of their country. They unreservedly accepted the new order and I never found that they held corporate views which ran contrary to the national interest. I never knew one who was not in a most genuine sense a lover of Ireland.[38]

O'Sullivan had a high regard for Keane:

Ever since the beginning he had proved himself to be, on the widest variety of subjects, a convincing and well-informed parliamentarian. He had originated debates on probably more occasions than any other member of the house, and he was a good debater as he was a public speaker.[39]

Keane contributed on a wide variety of topics including agricultural matters, the boundary commission, the rebuilding of the GPO, the Four Courts and the Custom House. He also made contributions on the Shannon hydro-electric scheme, compulsory Irish and the censorship of publications legislation, all of which he opposed. His opposition to the Shannon scheme was certainly idiosyncratic but his biographer in the *Dictionary of Irish biography* suggests that he considered the scheme to be socialistic and was unhappy with the granting of the contract to German engineers and with the estimated costs. Later he visited the Shannon and recorded: 'generally much impressed. The Germans are getting a firm hold, they have women and children, married quarters, engineers' houses, a school nearly finished ... the Irish appear to be doing only coolie work.'[40] With regards the Irish language, he supported it as an academic pursuit but he did not consider its revival to be realistic. Regarding censorship, he, like Yeats, wanted to retain a liberal, Protestant tradition and to resist the introduction of strict Roman Catholic morality into the law of the land. Yeats wrote him a letter saying how much he admired his speeches.

He spoke for nearly an hour on his own motion to reconstitute the Censorship of Publications Board after the banning of Eric Cross' *The Tailor and Ansty* and a number of other books on the grounds of obscenity in 1942. His quotations from *The Tailor and Ansty* had to be expunged from the record of the house and replaced by: 'Here the Senator quoted from the book'. He was a strong advocate of freedom of speech, stating:

If I were asked to choose between a united Ireland at the point of the Minister's blue pencil and 26 counties free to say what one likes, I would accept the latter every time. I don't think unity is worth anything if it were not going to have freedom of parliament, freedom of speech and freedom of the press.[41]

After a disturbance provoked by General Eoin O'Duffy's (1892–1944) National Guard ('Blueshirts') during the centenary celebrations of Mount Melleray in

1932, Keane opposed a ban on the organization: this probably did not indicate support but rather that a ban amounted to an infringement of civil rights.[42]

The minister for agriculture, Hogan, appointed Keane to the Agricultural Commission in 1922 and on its inauguration he wrote: 'I have not much confidence in the results; in any case commissions are out of place while all authority is usurped'.[43] However, he was to be a regular attender and contributor to its work.

In 1923 Keane wrote an article for *The Times* in which he referred to the Irish Land Bill:

> This is the Act so far as the 'cleaning up' of the land purchase is concerned. The terms are not generous, or even just, but, considering the circumstances of the case, they are merciful, and the Irish Government must be credited with doing its best to be just to a powerless and unpopular minority – a somewhat thankless task.

Shortly after Keane retired from the Senate, President Douglas Hyde (1860–1949) appointed him to the first Council of State. Further public service came when Keane, a director of the Bank of Ireland since 1926, was proposed as governor in 1928 but Ernest Blythe (1889–1975), minister for finance, objected. 'A bombshell to us all and I personally feel most unjust but not unexpected when we remember their conceit … I shall quit and get something in England.'[44] However, he did subsequently become governor. At this period the Bank of Ireland was effectively the state bank and played a key role in monetary policy prior to the establishment of the Central Bank of Ireland. Fellow senators Henry Guinness, himself a former governor of the Bank of Ireland, and Andrew Jameson were directors during Keane's tenure. He was also a director of Cement Limited.

During much of this time Keane was writing a weekly article for the *Sunday Times*, reporting on Irish issues such as politics, economics, the land problem, the Boundary Commission and the 'Blueshirts'.[45]

HOUSE BURNING

The outbreak of Civil War was to result in all members of the Free State legislature becoming targets of the Republican forces, who were opposed to the Anglo-Irish treaty. There were kidnappings and assassinations along with widespread destruction of business premises and homes by arson. Country houses were the particular target of arsonists. In January 1923 Keane records:

> As a senator I am warned to be discreet in my movements and I find I look around when crossing from the club to see if anybody is watching me. Similarly I take careful notice of people who follow me. I have asked

the club to take precautions by control of outside door ... It is hard to say where the political blood feud will end and how many innocent people will be swept into it. Until the people make sacrifices and take a firm hand the trouble will never end.[46]

Keane used the Kildare Street Club when in Dublin; later he was to purchase 47 Sandford Road as a Dublin home. The following month he and fellow senators had a meeting with General Richard Mulcahy (1886–1971), commander-in-chief of the National Army, regarding the protection of themselves and their property.[47] John Keane was well aware from the War of Independence that Cappoquin House might be a target and now his new role increased the risk. He wrote in his diary in February 1923: 'daily reports from Ireland of burning houses: ours must go in time'.[48] However, he had already taken precautions: by the summer of 1922 his wife and children were living in London where a house in Stafford Street was rented, and later they lived at 46 Hamilton Terrace. Previously, Keane had used the Army and Navy Club when in London.

Adele Keane wrote to her mother from Cappoquin in February 1922 telling of the packing of silver and china. The principal contents of the house were shipped to Bristol early in 1922 for storage with Lalonde, some were removed to John Palmer's of Waterford and some to Tivoli, the dower house on the Cappoquin estate. However, the contents of the library and some large items of furniture were to remain *in situ*. Palmer charged £149 13s. 9d. to transport two van loads and Lalonde charged four shillings per van, per week for storage.[49] Both Keane and his wife travelled to Bristol on separate occasions to inspect the storage facilities. When some of the original Tivoli furnishings were to be auctioned to make space, the auctioneer, Condon, advised against Keane's name being used.[50] This was a precaution to avoid making known that the main house was unoccupied and that furnishings were in storage at Tivoli. Keane wrote, following the removal of furniture, 'I do feel this is the beginning of our family's severance with Ireland.' Later he said that he was 'very much worried about the future: whether to stay in Ireland or not' and he considered letting the house for a period of seven years.[51] A further consignment of furniture was shipped to London in 1923; this probably had been stored in Tivoli from 1922.[52] The three best mantelpieces were removed in 1923 after a false report of the house being burned. Initially they were stored in the cellar at Cappoquin and later at Palmer's of Waterford. Keane halted their transport to England in 1923 when he began considering rebuilding: 'if I get a decree for rebuilding I may not send them to England at all'.[53] When in Waterford the family stayed either in Tivoli, their holiday home at Ardmore, or with neighbours following the emptying of their home, and its later destruction.

The destruction of castles and houses has always been a by-product of war and revolution. Ireland is no different and the 1798 Rebellion saw a spate of country house destruction with houses such as Blessington, Co. Wicklow, burned and the Bishop's Palace at Ferns ransacked in Co. Wexford. This pattern was to be repeated both in the War of Independence and in the Civil War. General Tom Barry (1897–1980) had declared that the homes of supporters of the crown were legitimate targets in the War of Independence.[54] In the Civil War the Republicans targeted all property belonging to supporters of the Anglo-Irish Treaty on the orders of Liam Lynch (1893–1923), commander-in-chief, issued in November 1922.[55]

There is no definitive figure for the number of houses destroyed between 1920 and 1923; however it is estimated by Terence Dooley to be close to 300 in the 26 counties that formed the Free State.[56] Seventy-six are known to have been destroyed in the War of Independence compared with almost 200 in the Civil War. The destruction of houses in the War of Independence was notably worse in Munster than in the other provinces: only a handful were attacked in Ulster, while the Civil War burnings were much more evenly distributed. The breakdown of law and order following the disbanding of the RIC accounts in part for the increased numbers during the Civil War.[57] These figures only include residences of landlords with more than 500 acres.

The motives for these burnings were numerous and are often difficult to ascertain; the stated reason may in fact hide something else. Dooley has enumerated a variety of reasons, which include political, military and agrarian issues. From 1920 to 1923 big houses were destroyed so that they could not be used as billets for crown forces, or for opposing forces in the Civil War, as reprisals for the owners giving support to the authorities, or as reprisals for the activities of British forces or the Free State government under public safety legislation.

In some incidents, such as the burning of Palmerstown House, Co. Kildare, the Republicans cited reprisals against the executions carried out by the Free State government under the Public Safety Act 1922 as a reason.[58] However, in many cases the legacy of agrarian grievances was a factor, not often stated; indeed the folk-memory of the response of certain landlords to the Famine may have been a factor in some cases.[59] Ciaran Reilly, who has studied house burning in Co. Offaly, is of the opinion that agrarian issues were the motivation in the majority of cases in that county. J.S. Donnelly has concluded that it was also a factor in Co. Cork. The destruction of the mansion house was likely to result in the estate being broken up and enhanced the chances of land redistribution.[60]

An interesting booklet entitled *Notes on the defence of Irish country houses,* which lacks any information as to its authorship or publication, survives in Ballindoolin, Co. Kildare, owned by the Tyrrell family. David Fitzpatrick has identified George O'Callaghan-Westropp (1864–1944), a Co. Clare landowner and a former army officer with previous experience of agrarian violence, as the author. It may have been produced following a resolution of the Clare Unionist Club seeking protection and when an outbreak of civil war 'such as may commence in the counties Cavan and Monaghan' was feared. The strategies outlined indicate the near impossibility of defending a country house:

Such a house, for effective resistance of a resolute and sustained attack, should be occupied by some fifty men, and it would take these at least forty-eight hours' incessant work, under skilled military direction, to enable them with reasonable hope of success to resist an attack, or series of attacks lasting for three days – a period which might elapse before military aid could arrive.[61]

This may have been intended to strengthen the case for the establishment of some form of state militia to protect private property.

January to March 1923 was the most destructive period for big houses and those burnt included homes of independent senators. On 9 January 1923 Marlfield, Co. Tipperary, the home of John Bagwell, was burned; on 29 January Palmerstown, Co. Kildare, the residence of the earl of Mayo, followed suit. Both were attacked by gangs of armed men and the occupants were given only minutes to leave. In both cases there was time to save a small amount of the furnishings. Kilteragh, Co. Dublin, home of Keane's great friend Sir Horace Plunkett, was mined on the same day as the fire at Palmerstown. Plunkett was absent but his staff rescued some furnishings.[62] In early February Moore Hall, Co. Mayo, the residence of Maurice Moore (although the property of his elder brother George), was burned with the total loss of its valuable contents. Desart Court, Co. Kilkenny, the home of the earl of Desart, the brother-in-law of Senator Ellen Cuffe, dowager countess of Desart, was destroyed on 22 February. Four days later Mullaboden, Co. Kildare, residence of General Bryan Mahon and his wife's family home, suffered the same fate. Mahon had removed some of the contents to Dublin for storage following the destruction of Palmerstown. On 16 March a large party of raiders attacked Ballynastragh, Co. Wexford. Thomas Grattan Esmonde, a Roman Catholic landlord, had moved to England and removed some of the contents. A land-mine caused serious damage to Castle Forbes, Co. Longford, seat of the earl of Granard and the Dublin house of Baron Glenavy, who was the chairman of the Senate, was burned. Oliver St John Gogarty lost both his family home at 5 Parnell Square, Dublin, and his country retreat, Renvyle, Co. Mayo, which was destroyed by a bomb.[63] Thomas Linehan of the Farmers' Party lost his house in Whitechurch, Co. Cork, and then Ballynahina, the farmhouse to which he had moved his family. Cavanore, Co. Louth, which Bernard O'Rourke, Cumann na nGaedheal, had recently bought from Thomas Jackson, was also destroyed.[64] Jane Wyse Power had her business premises burned and President Cosgrave's home, Beech Park, Rathfarnham, was attacked on 13 January 1923.

Plunkett, then in America, reflected to the *Irish Times* on his loss: 'While the house is a very fine one, the occurrence is not so regrettable as would have been the wrecking of some poor man's one-roomed dwelling.' At first Esmonde commented to the *Freeman's Journal* that 'the only reason for such an act is that I am a Senator of the Free State, and of course, I am in no worse a position than anybody else'. Later he wrote to a friend saying: 'After my burning I lost heart and gave up books altogether, so much so that I refused to accept books from several literary friends who wanted to give me their publications as I had no place to keep them.' He went on to say that he felt that his former work as a Nationalist MP should have been recognized and wrote to Cosgrave in June:

> I need not delay on the irreparable loss the destruction of such a home has been to me and mine; but I may state that we have never been voluntary absentees from our country; and we have done what we could in changeful conditions of Irish life for local development and improvement from generation to generation.[65]

In all, 37 senators lost property, of which 10 might be considered big houses.[66] However others such as Adare Manor, Co. Limerick (earl of Dunraven), Brownstown, Co. Kildare (Henry Greer), Burton Hall, Co. Dublin (Henry Guinness), Headfort, Co. Meath (marquess of Headfort), Heywood, Queen's County, now Co. Laois (William Hutchinson Poe), Randlestown, Co. Meath (Nugent Everard), Shelton Abbey, Co. Wicklow (earl of Wicklow), and Sutton House, Co. Dublin (Andrew Jameson) survived intact.[67] Dereen, Co. Kerry, seat of the marquess of Lansdowne, had been destroyed before his son, Henry Fitzmaurice, earl of Kerry, entered the Senate. Lady Lansdowne recorded that property, which had been looted, was returned after the intervention of the parish priest.[68] Desart, designed by Edward Lovett Pearce, with a magnificent carved wood staircase, was the greatest architectural loss and Marlfield contained a noted library.

19 FEBRUARY 1923

Cappoquin House was burnt on the night of 19 February 1923 (there had been a false report of Cappoquin burning on 14 December 1922) while Keane was in London. He learned of the burning by telegram on returning to Dublin and wrote in his diary on the evening of 20 February (fig. 7):

> on arrival learnt that Cap[poquin] Ho[use] had been burnt, main house completely destroyed, but servants' wing and stables escaped … It is sad to lose one's home where one's people have been for over 150 years and especially such a fine well decorated house … I am however spared to see the house used under some communal housing scheme or as a convent. It at least escapes such desecration. The incident brings to mind Lord Melbourne's advice 'do not try and do any good to people or you will only get into scrapes' … As one who was an advocate of greater political powers for a people who have proved themselves barbarians … However

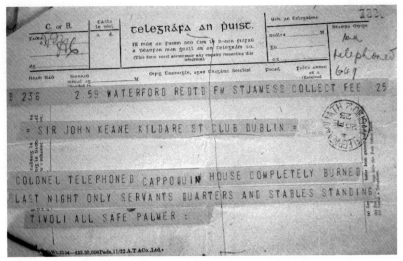

7. Telegram informing John Keane of fire, 20 February 1923.

if I had to live the past five years over again I would not have acted differently ... I only hope the British will not come back and save the wild men from the consequences of their folly. Nelly [Eleanor] will probably feel it more than I do and neither of us I trust will feel it more than our children who can grow up in other surroundings. I wish I was younger and could get work of some kind out of the country.[69]

Keane's reaction was quite measured but, like Esmonde, though he felt frustrated and betrayed by his fellow countrymen, he did not regret his actions. His comment regarding the possibility of his home becoming a convent may seem to be sectarian but this does not sit with his actions such as facilitating the establishment of a convent on his lands: it was probably a feeling of regret that a well-loved family home might become an institution of any kind. There is a hint that at that moment he felt there was no future for such houses or their owners; that they were destined to destruction or institutional use with their owners being forced to leave the country. To one sympathiser he replied: 'Thank you. But I expected it.'[70]

Keane had taken a strong line during the farm workers' strike in support of landowners. He had reluctantly accepted the treaty and committed himself to the Free State. This had led directly to the destruction of his home.

3. Cappoquin House: its destruction and rebirth

The architectural history of Cappoquin house is examined in this chapter and details of its reconstruction under John Keane's personal supervision are investigated. The fate of the homes of other independent senators will also be looked at.

It is necessary to examine the architectural history of Cappoquin House before considering its rebuilding after its burning in 1923. The names of both John Roberts (1712–96) and Davis Ducart (Dukart, Duckart or Daviso d'Arcort, died c.1780) have been proposed as the possible architect but no documentary evidence has come to light to confirm this.[1] The choice of the Waterford-based Roberts is entirely possible; he was architect of Moore Hall (1792), Co. Mayo, for George Moore; Tyrone House (1779), Co. Galway, for Christopher St George; and, uniquely, of both the Church of Ireland (1774) and Roman Catholic (1792) cathedrals in Waterford. The alternative candidate Ducart was both an architect and an engineer. His origins are unclear; he was probably from Piedmont in north-west Italy but is described as French by contemporaries. He is known to have collaborated with the Waterford architect Thomas Penrose on the Tyrone canal. He also used the Waterford stuccadore Patrick Osborne (who flourished in the 1760s and 1770s) to decorate at least three of his buildings including Castletown (1767), Co. Kilkenny, for Archbishop Michael Cox. Castletown is much admired today despite contemporary press accusations of Ducart being ignorant of the common rules and proportions of architecture.[2] While there is no documented work by him in Co. Waterford, it has been suggested by Desmond Fitzgerald that Castle Hyde (1750), also on the Blackwater near Fermoy, Co. Cork, might be his work.[3]

The relatively plain elevations of Cappoquin would fit into the *oeuvre* of either architect. Roberts was working at Curraghmore, Co. Waterford, and Ducart at Kilshannig, Co. Cork, around the period Cappoquin is thought to have been built. Both architects often feature slightly projecting central bays with a door surmounted by a fanlight and flanked by round-headed windows. If Ducart was the architect, then it is likely that the original Adamesque-style stucco decorations, now lost, were by Osborne. He is known to have undertaken comparatively minor commissions such as Ballycrenane, Co. Cork.[4]

The south front of Cappoquin, of approximately 70 feet, is seven-bay and two-storey faced in fine sandstone ashlar with limestone sills and is surmounted by a balustrade with boldly carved urns. The pale grey sandstone resembles limestone and has weathered well. The central three bays break forward slightly,

8. R. Armstrong, Belmont (Cappoquin House), 1843.

have arched windows at both levels, and an entrance door with a leaded fanlight. The east and west ends are of six bays, with the three southern bays projecting slightly and measure approximately 65 feet. The ashlar only extends round the three projecting bays. The west elevation had an iron or wooden veranda, added in the Regency period but replaced by a portico in the 20th century, around the door from the drawing room to the garden. The east elevation had a conservatory, probably added at the same time as the veranda, on its three southern bays. The plain north façade of six bays, and the back three bays of the side elevations, are of rubble stone and presumably were originally lime-rendered. An extensive service wing, some of which may pre-date the present house, is attached to the east end and the north side is enclosed by a stable court.[5] The ground floor plan of reception rooms on all four sides of a top-lit central staircase is repeated with bedrooms and dressing rooms on the first floor.[6] The south hall has a pillared-screen to the rear, a device first used in Ireland by Sir Edward Lovett Pearce (1699–1733) at Castletown, Co. Kildare; it was also used by Ducart at Castletown, Co. Kilkenny.[7]

There is little record of the house before the fire of 1923 save for an ink and wash drawing by R. Armstrong dated 1843 (fig. 8).[8] An unsigned note referring to the history of the house states that Italian craftsmen were employed between 1775 and 1780 and that it incorporated some of a previous house built by the

9. Drawing room, Vance mantelpiece.

Cooke family.[9] There was a tendency to attribute any high-quality architecture and design to foreign craftsmen before late-20th century research began to reveal the names of Irish craftsmen. The note was probably written by a member of the family and, if Ducart was the architect, it is possible that the family retained the memory of a foreigner being involved in the design. A few old, poor-quality photographs of the exterior show the house substantially as it is today except for the old conservatory and veranda.

There is no record of the original interior decoration of the house save for a tantalizing reference by Dickinson to figurative, plaster mural panels based on Robert Adam's work: 'In Waterford there seems to have been a highly skilled local school, and excellent specimens of their work exist at Cappoquin House'.[10] Three original marble mantelpieces survive, two are contemporary with the building and one, possibly slightly older and of exceptional quality, was brought from a Dublin house of the Vance family, probably 18 Rutland Square, in the late 19th century (fig. 9).[11] Marble chimneypieces were always highly valuable objects and it was not uncommon to move them from house to house. The dining room and former drawing room mantels are of carved statuary marble with columns and are inset with brocatel marble from Siena. The dining room one has a central panel of a wreath and oak leaves with urns above the columns

while the drawing room one has Ionic columns and a central panel depicting a
shepherd tending a goat and sheep with an obelisk and a cottage in the distance.
The Vance example, in the original hall, is of Carrara marble with *verde antico*
green marble insets and carved panels of the highest quality and could be of
Dublin or London manufacture. An almost identical mantel, but with porphyry
insets, is in 52 St Stephen's Green. The figurative panels are identical and
Christine Casey has identified the designs as derived from the Borghese vase.[12]

Keane, who was working in Dublin, wanted to know as much as possible
regarding the attack on the house. Miss L. Bell, of the Cappoquin estate office,
forwarded a report written by Edward Brady that gave a vivid picture of the
devastating damage.

> I was called by one of my children at 3 o'clock, he told me Sir John's house
> was on fire as he slept in the back room and saw the fire from the window
> … I then went up and when I arrived there the principal part of the front
> and back block was a blazing furnace, the roof gone and all the lofts and
> windows, with the exception of two at the west end over the portico …
> From what I hear an entrance was made through the study window [the
> smoking room according to Miss Bell] also Master Richard's work shop
> window was raised up and a hole burned in the floor about 4 feet and
> two prams burned, no other damage done there. There was two chairs put
> under the stairs going up to the nursery and set on fire but the stairs did
> not take fire … one of the soldiers told me the lower part of the house was
> not on fire but the top was all in one blaze when he arrived there… we are
> getting everything that is loose away.[13]

Miss Bell added:

> roof gone by 4.00 [a.m.], wind blew away from servants quarters …
> some damage to stone around windows … some interior brick partitions
> collapsed … decoration destroyed, slates destroyed, chimney pieces
> destroyed, tanks, lead pipes, copper pipes … conservatory escaped.

None of the remaining contents of the house was saved except for some
packing cases which were awaiting removal in the hall. There was little left to
loot but some furnishings of the servants' wing, including lace curtains, a mirror
and an axe, were taken.[14] Occupation of this wing by the National Army the day
after the fire resulted in some further damage and any remaining furniture had
to be moved to the old forge.[15]

Keane noted that his wife would probably feel the loss more than he did. It
was Eleanor Keane who wrote to the estate office three days after the fire and
before there is any record of her husband contemplating rebuilding. She clearly
envisaged complete restoration, writing: 'the great thing is to secure in a place

of safety <u>all</u> the building materials that can be used again' and she went on to suggest that Brady should buttress the walls if necessary. Three days later she asked Bell to get a sample of the blue-painted plaster on the walls of the south hall as 'the one I brought over fell to pieces so I am afraid the painters will hardly match the shade'.[16] This latter statement would indicate that she had travelled from London to visit the ruins immediately after the fire.

Waterford was a centre of considerable Republican activity and, even laying aside Keane's role as a senator, the empty Cappoquin House could have been seen as a military target given its potential use as a barracks. There is no known witness account of the attack on the unoccupied house but it is probable that only a small number of men were involved, unlike large raiding-parties who confronted owners or servants at some houses. It is certainly conceivable that animosity resulting from Keane's role in the farm workers' strike may have been a particular factor in this case, but it remains unproven as no specific reason for the burning was given at the time. R.V. Comerford has written that country houses:

> had been made into a symbol of oppression and decadence in order to justify the long land war, and the dominant party politics of the occupants was sufficient pretext to perpetuate the antipathy into the revolutionary years and beyond. Landlord and big house would do as synecdoche for all the historical grievances of the nationalist narrative.[17]

As the house was unfurnished, save for the library and some large items such as a grand piano and mirrors, there was little opportunity for looting, which was a concomitant factor in some cases. The estate office reported that a notice posted on the garden gate (presumably by the National Army), warning that persons found loitering on the premises would be severely dealt with and were liable to be shot, had been torn down and that rose bushes had been dug up and taken from the garden.[18]

Cappoquin House had been insured with London and Lancashire Insurance for £25,000 and the contents for £5,000. As insurance companies did not cover 'civil commotion' the protracted process of claiming compensation under the Damage to Property (Compensation) Act 1923 had to be used. Keane had been a contributor to the Senate debate introducing the bill.[19] In June 1923 the architect Page Dickinson and a surveyor, Graves Clayton, prepared a report to support a claim for £31,200, less £7,800, for partial re-use of the walls.[20] There were further claims for loss of furniture and books, earlier loss of livestock, and damage caused by army occupation. An inventory of library books had been made in 1922 and they were valued from this list by F.J. Fox of the London Library at £265 14s. 3d. after the fire.[21] Palmer provided valuations for the lost and damaged furniture and mahogany doors: 'grand piano £100, Chippendale carved wood mirror £100 … 7 mahogany doors £84, salvage £35'.[22] He considered that the doors could be repaired but it appears that they were in fact replaced.

Property owners could also make claims for damage resulting from civil disorder which occurred before July 1921 through the London-based Irish Grants Committee compensation legislation. The Free State introduced the Damage to Property Act for claims after July 1921. Keane was awarded £12,894 in 1923: approximately 55 per cent of Dickinson's submitted claim for £23,400.[23] It seems to have been the pattern that claims were only partially met as Esmonde received a similar percentage of his claim for Ballynastragh.[24] However, awards were higher if the owner intended to rebuild and were paid in increments as the project advanced. A small portion of the payment was in the form of 5 per cent Compensation Stock rather than cash.

PHOENIX ON THE BLACKWATER

As Dickinson had not resumed his Dublin-based partnership after war service and was working partly in London, probably due to economic reasons, he was not available to oversee the rebuilding. On 15 December 1923 Richard Caulfield Orpen, RHA (1863–1938), to whom Dickinson had served as an apprentice and later as a partner, was appointed architect at a rate of 5 per cent of the award or of the costs, whichever was the greater. A combination of special contracts and direct labour was agreed.[25] From time to time both Clayton and Orpen had to request payments from Keane as he often faced cash-flow problems due to the protracted system of incremental payment of compensation on completion of work and following site inspections by J.H. Williams from the Office of Works in Waterford.[26] There are records showing several different amounts of compensation granted but the figures below seem to be Keane's own record.

	Expenditure:	1924–25	£1,997 5s. 9d.
		1925–6	£2,380 5s. 1d.
		1926–27	£2,220 10s. 5d.
		1927–8	£1,842 8s. 6d.
		Total:	£8,440 9s. 9d.

Compensation received:	1925	£2,900 in three increments
	1926	£1,000
	1927	£4,000 in two increments
	Total:	£7,900 [27]

Awards were open to appeal by both parties and the burden of paying fell to county councils, who were reluctant to pay. Keane had probably excluded payments in government stocks and ancillary claims from his figures. There was an offer of £801 compensation for the occupation of Tivoli by the National

10. Reconstruction over drawing room.

Army.[28] The compensation award did not allow for the restoration of internal decoration: 'all ornamentation cut out – a scandal'. Such work would have accounted for a significant part of the costs.[29] The fact that Keane had an income from business interests, in addition to the farm, enabled him to make up any shortfall in funding, yet all ornamentation was left out in the billiards' room (former drawing room).

In 1926 Keane was still pursuing a claim to the Irish Grants Committee (British) for losses, including seven bullocks 'driven off my land and it is known locally that they were killed and eaten by republican soldiers', and stating that the loss was occasioned by his allegiance to the United Kingdom before 11 July 1921.[30] The Irish Grants Committee was established by the British government, with some funding from the Free State, to compensate southern loyalists who had fled Ireland and were effectively refugees. It was primarily for those in real hardship although some landowners did apply. It can be assumed that Keane would not have qualified as he had returned to Ireland and obtained compensation there.[31]

The Keanes were both fully involved in the planning and execution of the restoration. John acted as his own contractor through the Estate Company office – perhaps another example of his cautiousness in financial matters or his knowledge that the compensation would not be adequate (fig. 10). Edward Brady, a mason of 42 Barrack Street, Cappoquin, was his clerk-of-works, who, despite limited literacy, no formal training and an alcohol problem, showed great skill and was able to send rough sketches with accurate measurements to contractors in London in the absence of detailed working drawings from Orpen. He was even sent to a building exhibition in London. His skills were probably the reason why Keane was so tolerant of him and worked to keep the peace between him and the carpenter James Hackett.[32] If this was the same Hackett who worked on the 1913 redecoration of the drawing room, he also had a drink problem. During the war there had been a possibility that Brady might be discharged but Keane wrote to Eleanor: 'I have an idea you might like to use him on the tractor if you revive it. He has run a steam engine in the past ... pity to lose his building knowledge ... we must try and keep him.'[33]

Orpen restored the external appearance of the house, save for extending the parapet balustrade and urns on the south front around the entire roof. There was some fire damage to stone around the windows and doors and at least £190 was spent on new stone around the hall door and flanking windows. The original quarry must have been accessed as today any new stone has weathered and is indistinguishable from the original.[34] He did transfer the main entrance from the south to the north front and the north door and its flanking windows were given an entablature in composition stone; the other windows of this elevation were given similar architraves and the rubble stone was pointed rather than rendered (figs 11&12). Brady cast these items on site with a mixture of six-parts crushed stone to one-part Portland cement and then brushed the faces with a wire brush according to instructions supplied by the London-based Associate Portland Cement Manufacturers organization.[35] The conservatory was painted and re-glazed by Michael Regan at a cost of £9 10s. at this time but was reconstructed to a slightly different design some time later as can be seen by the 'shadow' of the original pitch of the roof on the wall of the house.

A major alteration, almost invisible due to the parapet balustrade, was the replacement of the pitched roof with a flat concrete one designed by Alfred Delap (1871–1943) of Delap and Waller, engineers. Delap's partner James de Warrenne Waller (1884–1968) was a pioneer in the use of ferro-concrete and had patented the 'Nofrango' system of light-weight concrete roofing used on blocks of flats being built for Dublin Corporation.[36] The concrete beams were also cast on site by the estate staff.

Estimates were sought from a number of suppliers for all phases of the work but, ultimately, all of the highly skilled decorative work went to London firms save for the library bookshelves and the staircase, which were made on site. It is notable that several Dublin firms were unable to supply items requested; this may reflect post-war shortages or a lack of large building projects due to the economic situation. However, Brooks Thomas, Maguire and Gatchell, and

11. Cappoquin House, south front.

12. Cappoquin House, north front.

T. and C. Martin of Dublin as well as Graves of Waterford provided much of the standard materials.[37] Keane demonstrated his continuing loyalty to the co-operative movement by instructing Brady to buy as far as possible from the local co-op.[38] A Thomson-Houston electric generator, 'practically new, lying at St Michael's, Dun Laoghaire', was acquired from J.P. Tierney.[39]

The highlight of the interior today is the fibrous plaster decoration, which was manufactured by G. Jackson & Sons of London and shipped over for installation.[40] Jackson also supplied embellished joinery for door architraves and window shutters. Other London suppliers were William Mallinson, who provided plywood faced with Cuban mahogany for the bookcases; Thomas Elsley, lead fanlights for the staircase hall and entrance doors; William Twigg, floor tiles and Kaye, door furniture. Pilkingtons of St Helen's glazed the windows and even some sanitary fittings came from George Jennings of London.[41] Keane, and frequently his wife Eleanor, visited these companies when in London and played an active role in the selection and design of all commissions.

The work of Jackson was the most significant and costly aspect of the new decorative scheme. A lack of interior photographs, referred to by Keane, was rather surprising for a large house at this period and made an accurate restoration of the original decorative scheme impossible.[42] While the dining room, drawing room (former front hall) and staircase hall were given Adam-style decoration, which presumably approximated to the original designs, different styles were used in other rooms. As in the redecoration of the drawing room in 1913, the Keanes' first instinct was to reproduce the lost decoration. Although he lacked a photographic record, Keane instructed Brady to salvage fragments of the original plasterwork, note their position in the house, and send them to Jackson.[43] Ultimately he abandoned this approach, probably due to the much higher cost of using bespoke moulds rather than stock designs. They opted for a variety of styles, perhaps suggested either by Jackson or Orpen, but reinstated Adamesque-detail in the principal spaces. A series of estimates from Jackson show the considerable cost of even stock designs. Invoices of £166 for the decoration of the octagon dome over the stairwell; £93 for the cornice frieze in the drawing room and £74 for the dining room; £55 for 12 sets of enriched architraves; £52 for two niches; and dado rail ranging from 1s. 8d. per foot to 2s. 10d. according to the degree of enrichment are examples of these costs.[44]

The three old mantels had suffered some damage either in removal or in storage and broken sections were sent to F.W. Smith of London to be copied. Some of the mouldings were simplified from egg-and-tongue to less-costly plain mouldings.[45] Repairs and loss of some decoration are visible on these chimney pieces today. The Keanes viewed antique mantelpieces in London for other rooms but finally they selected simple reproductions of classical designs, mainly in wood, for minor rooms and bedrooms from Bratt Colbran, P. Morley Horder and Caron and Company, London.[46] Those in the north hall and library were later replaced with antique marble ones, sourced locally by Keane's daughter-in-law, Olivia.

13. Dining room.

14. Library.

15. Billiard room, detail of mantelpiece.

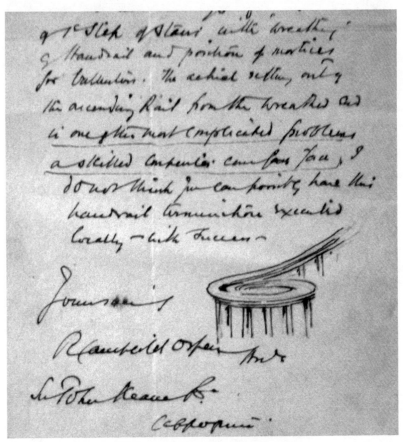

16. Richard Orpen, sketch for staircase.

The dining room had its mantel re-instated and the plasterwork includes a neo-classical frieze, a central Adam-style fan oval on the ceiling and a dado with erect-leaf decoration (fig. 13). The new drawing room has the Vance mantel, a frieze of ox skulls with swags, a large ceiling centre-piece incorporating arabesques and a dado rail with flutes and rosettes. The staircase hall with its dome incorporates Wedgewood-style figurative ovals with arabesques and swags. The new hall has a Corinthian cornice and a frieze with rococo decoration. A Doric cornice and frieze was used in the library (fig. 14) while the billiard room (fig. 15) (former drawing room) has only a simple cornice and a rococo ceiling rose – none of the decoration introduced earlier in the century was reproduced.

The most intricate works carried out on site were the library bookcases and the staircase, which are a tribute to the skills of Hackett and Brady.[47] There was much correspondence between Orpen and Eleanor Keane on the design of the library bookcases, which were constructed under Hackett's direction. She wanted sliding doors, however, they were constructed with hinged doors. The awkward skew-door from the staircase hall caused problems in relation to the fittings.[1] Orpen and Brady exchanged sketches on details of the construction of the stairs and banisters (fig. 16), which were also constructed by Hackett. The architect considered that the carving of the curved handrail terminator would be beyond Hackett's capabilities and the entire handrail was supplied by T. and C. Martin.[2] Garret Dalton of Ballingowan and Frank Dalton of Dungarvan were assistants to Hackett with the woodwork.[50]

The original mahogany doors appear to have been deemed too badly damaged to repair and Keane advertised in the *Irish Times* for antique doors.[51] No record has been found of the source of the doors used; however they must have been second-hand as they show signs of having been cut down to fit the openings. A Walter Bond of Newtownbond, Co. Longford, had responded to Keane's advertisement offering doors that he was prepared to take out of his house – an indication of the hard times then faced by the owners of large houses. Later, Keane himself was to comment on: 'The bad taste, decay and dilapidation' after visiting the Duckett family at Duckett's Grove and the Burtons at Burton Hall, both in Co. Carlow.[52]

'LONG AWAITED DAY'

The restoration by Orpen can be deemed a success and today the former hall makes a magnificent drawing room (fig. 17) while the new hall (fig. 18) and main entrance through the courtyard is equally attractive. The glazed doors linking the hall and staircase hall were probably an alteration but they bring much more sunlight into the interior. The standard of interior decoration is high and some of the plasterwork, notably on the staircase lantern (fig. 19), is spectacular. Purists may criticize the introduction of anachronistic decorative schemes in the north hall and library but few houses survive for over 200 years without some alterations. The innovative flat, concrete roof has stood the test of time save for some condensation problems on the top-floor ceiling, first noted during construction.[53] Major work was carried out in recent years but a traditional slate roof would have required similar maintenance. The composition stone manufactured on site for the decoration of the north front has also worn well and developed the patina of real stone.

The rebirth of the still uncompleted house, Keane's 'long awaited day', was marked by a coming-of-age dance for his son Richard held on 7 January 1930.[54] There were around 150 guests and temporary electric power had to be brought from the estate saw mill. Keane was delighted at how well the house looked and the sum of £149 was expended on the festivities. John Bagwell, ally of Keane in the Senate, who had been through the same saga of house destruction and

17. Drawing room.

18. Hall.

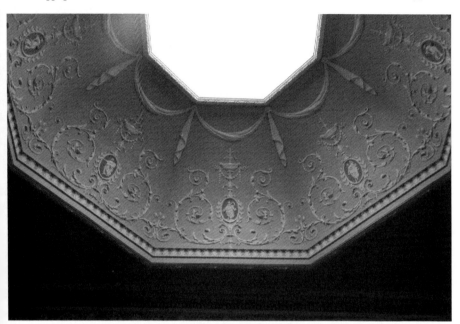

19. Lantern over staircase hall.

reconstruction at Marlfield, was among the guests celebrating Cappoquin's exemplary restoration.

It is significant that 90 per cent of the large houses owned by senators, that were destroyed or damaged, were rebuilt or restored: for example Cappoquin, Desart Court, also by Orpen (subsequently demolished), Marlfield, Palmerstown, and Mullaboden. Castle Forbes was restored and both Kilteragh and Renvyle were rebuilt in modified form while Ballynastragh was replaced by a new house. The planned restoration of Moore Hall never materialized and it is the only one that remained a ruin.[55] Overall, a much smaller percentage of houses destroyed in the period appear to have been rebuilt and Reilly has shown that only 20 per cent of the houses destroyed in King's County (now Co. Offaly) were rebuilt.[56] This is probably explained by the fact that the landlords who had accepted nomination to the Senate had already made a firm commitment to remain and adapt to the new order in Ireland. Robert O'Byrne has observed that Cappoquin is 'a rare instance of an Irish house resurrected after the Troubles' and today Castle Forbes and Cappoquin House stand out as the only country houses of those independent senators still occupied by their families.[57]

The compensation scheme for Civil War damage made the rebuilding of Cappoquin a long and tortuous process, which Keane pursued with customary determination. The rebuilt house has a finely decorated interior despite the compromises that had to be made.

Conclusion

John Keane has left an extensive record of his life through his diaries in which he made a relatively terse record of his daily activities, sometimes with little or no comment, but on other occasions with observations on the events and people encountered; very rarely he wrote a longer reflection. With the exception of a few comments in newspapers and Donal O'Sullivan's study of the Senate, there is little record of what his contemporaries thought of him.

It can be said that he lived up to his family's motto: '*Virtute* – By virtue', and to his own declaration, made at the age of 24, that his public life should be dedicated to 'my country and the welfare of my people first and principles and standards of public honesty first [*sic*]'.[1] This raises the question as to whether he is referring to the Irish people or the British people as a whole. At the time he wrote this he certainly meant the British people but as events unfolded it gradually came to be the Irish people and what he saw as being best for their future. Keane was not only honest and truthful in accord with his Christian principles but also in pursuing what he believed to be right, according to his own convictions, regardless of the consequences. He was also brave, as recognized twice on active military service and also as demonstrated by his service as a senator during the civil war.

A MAVERICK?

A man who could put Senator, Lieutenant-Colonel and Sir before his name and 5th baronet, barrister-at-law, mentioned in dispatches (South Africa), member of Waterford County Council, high sheriff of Co. Waterford, Distinguished Service Order, *Legion d'honneur*, mentioned in dispatches (First World War), governor of the Bank of Ireland and member of the Council of State after it might well be termed a maverick. The term, used by his biographer in the *Dictionary of Irish biography*, implies resistance to adherence to a group and if Keane's 'group' was the Protestant, Anglo-Irish then he can indeed be classed as a maverick as he did not adhere to the general views of the group which remained staunchly unionist. He clearly was one of several mavericks among those independent senators who might have been expected to put forward a common southern unionist position.

Keane had been born into the Protestant ascendancy and the path of his early life and his first political opinions followed a pre-ordained pattern. When he first considered a political career it was to have been as a unionist of some form, probably representing an English constituency, and definitely not as a nationalist. He gave the impression that he would have supported Gladstone on home rule but later felt that the land question had to be resolved before it could become a reality. His involvement with the co-operative movement, Waterford County Council and the Irish Farmers' Union brought him into the struggle between unionist and nationalist and made him acutely aware of the realities of the situation. Ultimately, as for Plunkett, O'Brien and Redmond, the tide of nationalism was moving too fast for those like Keane who were advocating a middle way. He clung to the ideal of an all-island, self-governing dominion within the British empire but was pragmatic enough to accept the reality of the Irish Free State even if it was not what he would have desired. Donal O'Sullivan observed: 'There was a certain rugged stoicism in his nature, doubtless derived from his northern ancestry ... the leading characteristic was his energetic individualism, a boyish trait without taint of selfishness or pomposity.'[2] There are indications that Keane's Achilles' heel was his inability to work with others and this may have limited his influence in the various causes he espoused during his life. O'Sullivan felt that: 'His great defect lay in his unwillingness to co-operate with any group or party'.[3]

Keane's decision to remain in Ireland after 1922, to take part in its public and business life and to rebuild Cappoquin House was exceptional. Many Protestant landowners left for England and those that remained tended to keep a low profile and avoid politics at any level. Reflecting in 1933, in an address to the London-based Royal Institute of International Affairs (Chatham House), he said: 'But in all the circumstances a powerless minority have every reason to be grateful for the buffer these men [W.T. Cosgrave, Kevin O'Higgins and Patrick McGilligan] interposed between the popular cupidity and vested interests. In many cases treatment was generous.'[4]

Keane's career was to keep him away from home for extended periods but he appears to have enjoyed a happy marriage. His almost daily letters to Eleanor during the First World War are very affectionate and full of praise for her management of family and estate. When he was in London on leave she always travelled to meet him and later when his family had to live in London he commuted almost weekly to visit them. He remembered his children's birthdays, even when far from home, and frequently enquired of Eleanor as to their progress.

Keane was conscious that he was not Anglo-Irish like a majority of the ascendancy and was acutely aware of his family's Gaelic, Catholic origins. In a Senate speech he said: 'Does he realise that in my blood there is a record of knowledge of confiscation and oppression just as great as in any member of this House? My ancestors were driven out of the O'Cathain country by the British in the Elizabethan days.' While he may have wavered in his commitment to Ireland at times of danger, in particular to his family, he never wanted to abandon Ireland for Britain. For him, Ireland was his family's homeland and not just a 'picnic in a foreign land', an attitude Edith Somerville (1858–1949) ascribed to her fictional Anglo-Irish characters.[5] It was notable that the English-born Eleanor Keane, who presumably had lived in Ireland as a young girl when her father was chief secretary, never seems to have considered leaving.

Keane's rebuilding of Cappoquin House was an act of faith and, as Elizabeth Bowen (1899–1973) wrote, it would have to discover a new future: 'The big house has much to learn – and it must learn if it is to survive at all'.[6] This big house, or its successive owners, did find a new future and it now welcomes visitors to house and garden where cultural events are hosted. Today the great houses of the Blackwater valley have found a role in their community and play a significant part in local tourism and the tensions of a century ago have receded into history.

Perhaps the words of the epitaph on Sir John Keane's memorial plaque in St Anne's parish church, Cappoquin, which read: 'With no thought for himself he served his country through war and peace', should be the final words on this remarkable man whose singular contribution to modern Irish history deserves to be better known.[7]

Notes

ABBREVIATIONS

ADC   aide-de-camp
DIB   J. Maguire and J. Quinn (eds), *Dictionary of Irish Biography* (Cambridge, 2009)
DSO   Distinguished Service Order
GPO   General Post Office
IAA   Irish Architectural Archive
IAOS   Irish Agricultural Organization Society
IAWS   Irish Agricultural Wholesale Society
IFU   Irish Farmers' Union
IGS   Irish Georgian Society
IRA   Irish Republican Army
ITGWU   Irish Transport and General Workers' Union
MP   Member of Parliament
NAI   National Archives of Ireland
OPW   Office of Public Works
RA   Royal Academy of Arts
RFA   Royal Field Artillery
RHA   Royal Hibernian Academy
RIC   Royal Irish Constabulary
UCC   University College Cork

Sir John Keane maintained a diary for most of his life. With one exception they are not in annual diaries but in notebooks that contain entries covering various time periods. There is break from 1914 to 1922; however the years 1914–19 are covered by almost daily letters to Lady Eleanor Keane. Unless otherwise specified in the notes, manuscripts cited are all in a private archive.

INTRODUCTION

1 *Cappoquin: a brief guide to an area's rich heritage* (Cappoquin Heritage Group, 2007) refers to an archaeological dig carried out by UCC in the 1980s (www. cappoquin.net/images/book/Book.pdf) (accessed 20 Oct. 2013).
2 Patrick C. Power, *History of Waterford: city and county* (Dublin, 1990), p. 65.
3 Diary of Sir John Keane, 26 Mar. 1897.
4 John Bateman, *Great landowners of Great Britain and Ireland* (London, 1883, repr. New York, 1970), p. 247.
5 John O'Hart, *Irish pedigrees, or, The origin and stem of the Irish nation* (Dublin, 1887), pp 495–6.
6 MS note re. history of Keane family and Cappoquin House, unsigned and undated; probably late 19th or early 20th century.
7 O'Hart, *Irish pedigrees*, pp 495–6 and MS family history copied from the Registry of Deeds, Dublin.
8 John Bernard Burke, *A genealogical and heraldic dictionary of the peerage and baronetage of the British Empire* (15th ed., London, 1853), p. 564 and O'Hart, *Irish pedigrees*, pp 495–6.
9 Diary, 15 Mar. 1897, 23 Jan. 1898 and letter from John Keane to Adelaide Keane, 6 Apr. 1897.
10 Patrick Maume, 'Keane, Sir John' in *DIB* (www.dib.cambridge.org.jproxy.nuim. ie) (accessed 22 May 2013).

I. JOHN KEANE AND HIS CONTEXT

1 Military records (www.sandhurst collection.org.uk) (accessed 22 May 2013).
2 Diary, 23 June 1899.
3 William Dalrymple, *Return of a king* (London, 2013).
4 Newspaper cuttings album, *Waterford Star*, 2 May 1899.
5 *Munster Express*, 3 Feb. 1956.
6 Diary, 11 Jan. 1899.
7 Diary, 5 Aug. 1897.
8 Diary, 21 May 1897.
9 Tour brochure of The Royal English Arboricultural Society and diary entry following tour, 18–20 Sept. 1913.
10 Diary, 25 July 1921.
11 Dairy, 14 Oct. 1924.
12 Diary, 2–5 Nov. 1899.
13 Diary, 11–12 Nov. 1899, 15 Nov. 1899 and 10 Dec. 1899.
14 Diary, 12 Dec. 1900.
15 Diary, 'The hole in this diary is made by a Boer bullet – it was lying just where I had a few moments previously been seated', 21 June 1900.
16 Letter, Keane to Adelaide Keane.
17 Diary, 14 Jan. 1900.
18 Keane's orders and medals. Private collection.
19 Diary, 21 Sept. 1900.
20 Richard Hawkins, 'Blake, Sir Henry Arthur' in *DIB*.
21 July 1909.
22 Power, *History of Waterford*, pp 197–9.
23 Printed letter, Richard Keane to his tenants, 14 Oct. 1881.
24 Power, *History of Waterford*, pp 201–3.
25 *Munster Express*, 10 Jan. 1930 (www. irishnewsarchive.com.jproxy.nuim.ie) (accessed 24 May 2013).
26 Census of Ireland, 1901, (www.census. nationalarchives.ie) (accessed 27 June 2013).
27 Diary, 20 Mar. 1897.
28 Diary, 18 Mar. 1897, 20 Nov. 1998, 6 Apr. 1899 and 26 July 1901. 'M' was possibly Mabel Dickinson.
29 Diary, 3 May 1899 and 7 May 1899.
30 Scott Morton, Tyncastle, Edinburgh, 1911, Ralph Havill, 31 Perry Street, Bristol, Feb. and Mar. 1911; John Palmer, 3 Catherine Street, Waterford, 12 Dec.

1911; and Wood & Gregory, 372 Euston Road, London, 6 Dec. 1911.
31 IAA, *Dictionary of Irish architects* (www. iarc.ie) (accessed 31 Oct. 2013) and Page Lawrence Dickinson to Keane, 24 July 1913, Keane to Dickinson, 25 Jan. 1914, and Dickinson to Keane, 4 Feb. 1914.
32 John Ryan, 28 Upper Abbey Street, Dublin, 30 May 1913, G. Jackson & Sons, Rathbone Place, London, 30 May 1913 and M. Creedon, Clare Lane, Dublin, 14 Apr. 1913. Keane to Dickinson, 11 Aug. 1913, 'I want the old work reproduced exactly in detail' and Dickinson to Keane, 14 Aug. 1913, 'I still think that the centres of the ovals should be at the same level – even if this is not a correct restoration'. Thomas Ulick Sadleir and Page Lawrence Dickinson, *Georgian mansions of Ireland* (Dublin, 1915).
33 J.W. Daly, 20 Jan. 1913.
34 Diary, 15 May 1913 and 31 Aug. 1923.
35 Diary, 25 Mar. 1897.
36 Power, *History of Waterford*, p. 136.
37 MS census return, 1891.
38 Diary, 16 May 1897.
39 Diary, 20 Apr. 1899.
40 Newspaper cuttings album, *Waterford Star*, 1894.
41 Ibid., 25 Aug. 1894.
42 Diary, 13 July 1895 and 26 June 1899.
43 Diary, 16 Dec. 1898.
44 Diary, 7 May 1897.
45 Dairy, 15 Aug. 1899.
46 Diary, 17 May 1897.
47 Diary, 14 Dec. 1897.
48 Diary, 4 June 1912; *Irish Times*, 15 Feb. 1913.
49 Diary, 3 June 1897.
50 Diary, 'If I had to make up my mind tomorrow in which interest to stand for parliament I would be in such difficulty that I am glad the opportunity not present.' 15 Aug. 1899.
51 Diary, 20 Feb. 1914.
52 Diary, July 1914.
53 Diary, 29 July 1914.
54 Newspaper cuttings album, poster, Waterford County Council election results, 1 June 1911.
55 Michael McDonagh, *The life of William O'Brien* (London, 1928), p. 185.
56 Newspaper cuttings album, *Cork Free Press*, undated (1910).

57 Newspaper cuttings album, 21 Mar. 1914.
58 Diary, 10 Feb. 1918.
59 Diary, 16 Aug. 1912.
60 Diary, 6 Aug. 1914 and 12 Aug. 1914.
61 Bureau of Military History, witness
    statement of Michael V. O'Donoghue,
    Lismore (www.bureauofmilitaryhistory.
    ie) (13 Oct. 2013).
62 Keane to Eleanor Keane, 13 Jan. 1915.
63 Keane to Eleanor Keane, 10 Nov. 1914, 14
    Jan. 1915, 17 Jan. 1915 and Apr. 1915.
64 Keane to Eleanor Keane, 7 Jan. 1914,
    Dec. 1914 and Apr. 1915.
65 Keane to Eleanor Keane, 4 Nov. 1914 and
    28 Apr. 1915.
66 Keane to Eleanor Keane, Apr. 1915.
67 Keane to Eleanor Keane, Nov. 1914.
68 Keane to Eleanor Keane, 16 Apr. 1915
    and 17 Apr. 1915.
69 Diary, 4 Aug. to 12 Sept. 1914.
70 Citation, mentioned in dispatches, 30
    Nov. 1915 and Citation, DSO, 1 Jan.
    1916. Keane to Eleanor Keane, 6 June
    1917.
71 *Irish Times*, 6 Aug. 1914
72 Keane to Eleanor Keane, 30 Apr. 1916.
73 Keane to Eleanor Keane, 2 July 1916 and
    Times, 1 July 1916.
74 Keane to Eleanor Keane, 9 Aug. 1917.
75 Keane to Eleanor Keane, Feb. 1915, Mar.
    1915, Apr. 1915, and 3 June 1917.
76 Keane to Eleanor Keane, 24 Feb. 1915.
77 Keane to Eleanor Keane, 10 Apr. 1916.
78 Keane to Eleanor Keane, 2 Nov. 1914.
79 Keane to Eleanor Keane, 1915.
80 Keane to Eleanor Keane, 15 Mar. 1919.

2. WARS AND REVOLUTION AT HOME

1   David Fitzpatrick, 'The geography of
    Irish nationalism', *Past and Present*, 78
    (Feb. 1978), 116–22.
2   Bureau of Military History, witness
    statements of Thomas Kelleher,
    Cappopquin and Michael V.
    O'Donoghue, Lismore (www.
    bureauofmilitaryhistory.ie) (accessed 13
    Oct. 2013).
3   Diary, 28 May 1921.
4   Diary, 10 June 1921.
5   Diary, 13 July 1921 and 7 Dec. 1921.
6   Diary, 17 Jan. 1922.
7   Diary, 1 June 1922 and 6 June 1922.
8   *Irish Times*, 19 Jan. 1923.

9   Diary, 2 June 1922.
10 Diary, 28 June 1922 and 30 June 1922.
11 Diary, 10 Aug. 1922 and 11 Aug. 1922.
12 Diary, 1 July 1922.
13 Diary, 23 Aug. 1922.
14 Diary, 4 Nov. 1922.
15 David Fitzpatrick, *Politics and Irish life,
    1913–1921: provincial experience of war and
    revolution* (Cork, 1997), pp 221–3.
16 Power, *History of Waterford*, p. 233.
17 Ibid., pp 243–6.
18 Diary, 7 June 1922.
19 Diary, 8 June 1922.
20 Diary, 9 June 1922 and *Irish Independent*,
    23 June 1923.
21 Diary, 22 Jan. 1922.
22 Diary, 13 June 1922 and 16 June 1922.
23 Diary, 15 June 1922, 16 June 1922, 21 June
    1922, 26 June 1922 and 3 Aug. 1922.
24 Scrapbook, press cuttings, photographs
    of the *Lady Belle* being unloaded at
    Dungarvan, 11 June to 21 July 1923.
25 Diary, 20 June 1922.
26 *Irish Independent*, 23 June 1923.
27 Diary, 19 Aug. 1922.
28 Power, *History of Waterford*, p. 248.
29 Diary, 15 Dec. 1921.
30 *Irish Independent*, 19 June 1923 and 28 June
    1923.
31 Ibid., 1 Oct. 1923.
32 Diary, 3 July 1922.
33 Scrapbook, speech to county Waterford
    branch of IFU, Feb. 1924.
34 Scrapbook, newspaper cutting 'Keane's
    battered halo', *Voice of Labour*, 12 Aug.
    1923.
35 Diary, 24 Jan. 1923 and 13 Apr. 1923.
36 Ulick O'Connor, *Sunday Independent*, 3
    Apr. 2011.
37 Scrapbook, untitled newspaper cutting,
    July 1923.
38 Donal O'Sullivan, *The Irish Free State
    and its senate: a study in contemporary politics*
    (London, 1940), p. 130.
39 Ibid., p. 180.
40 Maume, 'Keane, Sir John' in *DIB*; Diary,
    26 Aug. 1926.
41 Diary, 11 April 1929
42 Power, *History of Waterford*, pp 265–6.
43 Diary, 2 Nov. 1922.
44 Diary, 27 Mar. 1928.
45 Scrapbook, newspaper cuttings, *Sunday
    Times*, 1925–35.
46 Diary, 15 Jan. 1923.

47 Diary, 23 Jan. 1923 and 8 Feb. 1923.
48 Diary, 5 Feb. 1923.
49 Adele Keane to Eleanor Keane, 23 Feb.
    1922, 'packers began yesterday and have
    done a good deal of the china'. John D.
    Palmer, Waterford, 22 Mar. 1922.
50 Diary, 20 Jan. 1922.
51 Diary, 21 Feb. 1922 and 9 June 1922.
52 Invoice, Palmer May 1923.
53 Keane to Edward Brady, 'remove
    mantelpieces in drawing room, front hall
    and back hall ... I don't want anyone to
    know', 20 Jan. 1923 and Keane to Palmer,
    20 Sept. 1923.
54 Ciaran J. Reilly, 'The burning of
    country houses in county Offaly during
    the revolutionary period, 1920–23'
    in Terence Dooley and Christopher
    Ridgeway (eds), *The Irish country house, its
    past, present and future* (Dublin, 2011),
    p. 117.
55 Terence Dooley, *The decline of the big house
    in Ireland: a study of Irish landed families,
    1860–1960* (Dublin, 2001), p. 237.
56 Terence Dooley 'National patrimony and
    political perceptions of the Irish country
    house' in Terence Dooley (ed.), *Ireland's
    polemical past* (Dublin, 2010), p. 195.
57 Terence Dooley, *The big houses and landed
    estates in Ireland; a research guide* (Dublin,
    2007), p. 135.
58 Dooley, *The decline of the big house in
    Ireland*, p.175.
59 Ibid., pp 171–207.
60 Reilly, 'The burning of country houses
    in county Offaly' in Dooley and
    Ridgeway (eds), *The Irish country house,
    its past, present, and future* p. 118; J.S.
    Donnelly Jr, 'Big House burnings in
    county Cork during the Irish revolution,
    1920–21', *Eire-Ireland*, 47:3 & 4 (2012),
    141–97.
61 *Notes on the defence of Irish country houses*,
    unsigned and undated, pp 2–3; *Kildare
    Observer*, 28 July 1920 and 14 Aug. 1920;
    Fitzpatrick, *Politics and Irish life*, p. 60.
62 *Freeman's Journal*, 10 Jan. 1923 and *Irish
    Independent*, 31 Jan. 1923.
63 *Freeman's Journal*, 6 Feb. 1923, 17 Feb.
    1923, 19 Feb. 1923, 24 Feb. 1923 and 17
    Mar. 1923.
64 *Freeman's Journal*, 19 Feb. 1923 and
    Donegal News, 24 Feb. 1923.

65 *Freeman's Journal*, 12 Mar. 1923. Sir
    Thomas Esmonde to Lord Eversely,
    NAI, Esmonde papers, quoted by
    Dooley in *The decline of the big house in
    Ireland*, p. 190 and Sir Thomas Esmonde
    to W.T. Cosgrave, NAI, Esmonde
    papers, quoted by Dooley in ibid., p. 193.
66 Dooley, *The decline of the big house in
    Ireland*, p. 190.
67 Bence-Jones, Mark, *A guide to Irish
    country houses* (London, 1988), pp 1–2,
    150–2, 237, 259 and 268.
68 Diary, 15 Sept. 1923.
69 Diary, 13 Dec. 1922 and 20 Feb. 1923.
70 Scrapbook, cutting, letter to the editor
    the *Irish Times* from Donal O'Sullivan, 4
    Feb. 1956.

3. CAPPOQUIN HOUSE: ITS DESTRUCTION AND
REBIRTH

1   The attribution to Roberts appears to
    be long-standing; the suggestion of
    Ducart comes from David J. Griffin,
    former Director IAA in IAA, *Dictionary
    of Irish architects, 1720–1940* (www.
    iarc.ie, accessed 31 Oct. 2013) and in
    conversation with author.
2   Quoted in IAA, *Dictionary of Irish
    architects, 1720–1940* from *Sleater's Public
    Gazetteer*, Nov. 1769 and *Freeman's
    Journal*, 2–4 Feb. 1773.
3   Desmond Fitzgerald, Knight of Glin,
    'The architecture of Davis Ducart',
    Country Life, 142 (5 Oct. 1967), 738–9.
4   John Logan, 'Dropped into this kingdom
    from the clouds: the Irish career of Davis
    Dukart, architect and engineer, 1761–81',
    Irish Architectural and Decorative Studies, 10
    (2007), 57–9.
5   Bence-Jones, *A guide to Irish country
    houses*, p. 56. MS ground plan, unsigned,
    undated and author's observations.
6   MS ground floor plan, 8 feet to 1 inch,
    unsigned, undated, probably Page
    Dickinson, post-1923 fire.
7   Bence-Jones, *A guide to Irish country
    houses*, pp 75–7.
8   R. Armstrong, an unrecorded artist,
    probably an amateur. Private collection.
9   MS note re. history of Keane family and
    Cappoquin House.
10 Sadleir and Dickinson, *Georgian mansions
    in Ireland*, p. 8.

11 John Keane's mother was Adelaide Vance. The Vance family owned 18 Rutland Square and a house in Merrion Square, Dublin, in the 18th and 19th centuries.

12 J.P. Mahaffy, R.C. Orpen and W.G. Strickland (eds), *The Georgian Society records* (Dublin, 1910, repr. Shannon, 1969), plate LVI and Christine Casey, *The buildings of Ireland: Dublin* (New Haven and London, 2005), p. 542.

13 MS report by Edward Brady, undated (Feb. 1923).

14 Bell to Keane, 7 Mar. 1923.

15 Palmer to Keane, 22 Feb. 1923.

16 Eleanor Keane to Bell, 23 Feb. 1923 and 26 Feb. 1923.

17 R.V. Comerford, 'Foreword' in Terence Dooley and Christopher Ridgway (eds), *The Irish country house; its past, present and future* (Dublin 2011), p. 11.

18 Estate Office to Keane, 7 Mar. 1923.

19 Diary, 12 Apr. 1923.

20 Page L. Dickinson, report on damage to Cappoquin House, June 1923 and letters, Department of Finance to Keane, 27 Feb. 1923 and 17 Feb. 1927.

21 Library catalogue with valuations by F.J. Fox, London Library, 22 Sept. 1924.

22 Palmer to Keane, 1923.

23 Dooley, *The decline of the big house in Ireland*, pp 203–4.

24 Orpen to Keane, 13 Dec. 1923 and 15 Dec. 1923.

25 Keane to Orpen, 13 Dec. 1923

26 J. Graves Clayton to Keane, 14 July 1924 and Keane to J.H. Williams, 2 Apr. 1928.

27 MS account, unsigned, undated, probably Keane.

28 OPW to Keane, 17 May 1924.

29 Diary, 19 May 1924, 'all ornamentation cut out – a scandal'.

30 Keane to Irish Grants Committee, 3 Dec. 1926.

31 N. Brennan, 'Minefield: southern loyalists, the Irish Grants Committee and the British government, 1922–1931', *Irish Historical Studies*, 3:119 (1997).

32 Census of Ireland 1911 (www.census. nationalarchives.ie, accessed 27 June 2013). Keane to Estate Office, Apr. 1928; Diary, 30 Oct. 1925, 'Brady has been drinking on the job' and Census of

Ireland 1911, Luke and James Hackett, carpenters, 18 Green Street, Cappoquin (www.census.nationalarchives.ie, accessed 27 June 2013).

33 Keane to Eleanor Keane, 5 Jan. 1918.

34 Clayton account, Mar. 1924.

35 The Associate Portland Cement Manufacturers, Tothill Street, London.

36 Diary, 18 June 1924. IAA, *Dictionary of Irish architects, 1720–1940* (www.iarc.ie, accessed 2 July 2013).

37 Brooks Thomas, Sackville Place; Maguire & Gatchell, 10 Dawson Street; T. & C. Martin, D'Olier House and 82 North Wall; Graves, Waterford.

38 Keane to Brady, 13 Feb. 1928.

39 J.P. Tierney & Company, 44 Kildare Street, to Keane, 25 Oct. 1928.

40 G. Jackson & Sons, 41 Rathbone Place, London.

41 William Mallinson & Sons, Hackney Road, London, 29 Dec. 1928; Thomas Elsley, Titchfield Street, London, 9 Feb. 1928; William H. Twigg & Son, Upper Thames Street, London, 27 Dec. 1928; Kaye & Sons, High Holborn, London, 24 Dec. 1928 and George Jennings, 63–7 Lambeth Palace Road, London.

42 Diary, 20 Feb. 1923, 'I now wish I had good interior photographs'.

43 Keane to Brady, 13 Nov. 1926.

44 Jackson, 19 Dec. 1927, 25 Oct. 1928, 29 Mar. 1928 and 8 May 1929.

45 F.W. Smith, 176 York Road, London, 23 Dec. 1929.

46 Diary, 11 May 1924. Crowther, North End Road, London, Bratt Colbran & Co., 10 Mortimer Street, London, P. Morley Horder, Arlington Street, London and Messrs Caron Co, 9 Wells Mews, London.

47 A diary entry by Keane dated 29 April 1927 mentions a meeting with 'Hicks' in Dublin in 1927 and later 'authorised Hicks to proceed'. This raises the possibility that the Dublin cabinetmaker James Hicks might have tendered for some aspect of the work, most likely the library. There is no evidence of any of his work in the house, nor is there any correspondence or invoices extant.

48 Orpen to Eleanor Keane, 27 Sept. 1928 and 28 Dec. 1928.

49 Orpen to Brady, 19 Mar. 1928 and Orpen to Keane, 12 Mar. 1928. T. & C. Martin, 13 Dec. 1929.
50 Scrapbook, press cutting, untitled, 28 Dec. 1929.
51 *Irish Times*, 28 Dec. 1923.
52 Diary, 14 July 1928.
53 Diary, 15 Mar. 1927, 'a lot of damp under roof'.
54 Diary, 7 Jan. 1930.
55 Bence-Jones, *A guide to Irish country houses*, pp 26, 56, 67, 103, 177, 203, 210–11, 220, 230, 241.
56 Reilly, 'The burning of country houses in county Offaly during the revolutionary period. 1920–23' in Dooley and Ridgeway (eds), *The Irish country house its past, present and future*, pp 110–11.
57 Robert O'Byrne, 'Rebuilding Cappoquin', *Irish Arts Review* (Spring 2013), 133–5.

CONCLUSION

1 Diary, 16 May 1897.
2 Scrapbook, cutting, letter to the editor the *Irish Times* from Donal O'Sullivan, *Irish Times*, 4 Feb. 1956.
3 O'Sullivan, *The Irish Free State and its Senate*, p. 180.
4 Scrapbook, 2 Mar. 1933.
5 Ann Morrow, *Picnic in a foreign land: the eccentric lives of the Anglo-Irish* (London, 1989), title from Edith Somerville and Martin Ross, *Some experiences of an Irish RM*.
6 Elizabeth Bowen, 'The big house', *The Bell*, 1:1 (Oct. 1940), 71–7.
7 Memorial plaque in Cappoquin Church of Ireland church. Epitaph probably composed by his son Richard Keane.